Astrology for Self-Healing:

The Essential Guide

Alan Richards-Wheatcroft

Copyright 2018 by Alan Richards Wheatcroft
No part of this book may be reproduced or transcribed in any form or by any means, electronic or mechanical, including photocopying or recording or by any information storage and retrieval system without written permission from the author and publisher, except in the case of brief quotations embodied in critical reviews and articles. Requests and inquiries may be mailed to: American Federation of Astrologers, Inc., 6535 S. Rural Road, Tempe, AZ 85283.

ISBN-13: 978-0-86690-672-2

Editor: Paul F. Newman
Cover Design: Jack Cipolla

Published by:
American Federation of Astrologers, Inc.
6535 S. Rural Road
Tempe, AZ 85283

Contents

Foreword	ix
An Important Message from the Author	xi
Proof that Astrology Actually Works	xiii
Welcome to the Age of Aquarius	xv
Preface	xix
Astrology: A Universal Language	xxv
Astrology: Changing Politics	xxvii

Part 1: Preliminaries

Chapter 1, An Ancient Belief System	1
Chapter 2, Universal Law	21
Chapter 3, Developing Dis-eases	33

Part 2: Prognosis

Chapter 4, The Counterpoint Effect	69
Chapter 5, Lunar Causality	97
Chapter 6, Healing via the Application of Color	117
Chapter 7, Predominant Healing Aspects	127
The Conjunction: Unification	
The Sextile: Expedience	
The Square: Stimulus	

Part 3: Prevention

Chapter 8, Evolutionary Memory	139
Chapter 9, Sleep Deprivation	149
Chapter 10, The Importance of Herbs, Vitamins and Minerals	159
Chapter 11, The Human Prime Directive	189
Chapter 12, A Guided Meditation: Healing the Mind, Body and Soul	193
Additional Publications by Alan Richards Wheatcroft	
Other Titles Published by AFA	
Astrology for Self-Healing	iii

Acknowledgements

"Be the change we wish to see in the world"—Mahatma Gandhi

In Divine Recognition of...

... My Spirit Guides, the Members of my Soul Group, the Angelic Host (the spiritual mainframe of the universe). Also, my Venusian Guardian Angel, symptomatic of Venus being exactly conjunct my Ascendant in the twelfth house; who coexists on the Earth plane and who applies hidden protection, guidance and love, thus imbuing me with God-light energy.

Joseph and the Persian Gentleman (highly evolved spirit guides). From them I receive spiritual guidance, wisdom, insight, beautifully-coordinated astrological knowledge, unconditional love, and the pivotal and climacteric information that has made this publication possible.

Everlasting Love and Eternal Blessings!

In Remembrance of...

Diana Pope, for being an unprecedented "pillar of support." Your kindness never went *unnoticed*. More importantly, thank you for being a true, humble, and understanding friend and more importantly a soul companion. Live long and prosper!

Marilyn Archibald, it is with heartfelt thanks that I acknowledge the friendship we forged together, and for the support and wisdom you had freely given. God bless you on your journey through the spirit world.

Caroline Heaney, the original creator and the proprietor of the *Elfin*. Thank you for giving me that much-needed opportunity that successfully commenced my career in the field of astrological writing and esoteric study. With that said I hope that you acquire heartfelt peace, unconditional love and endless joy now that your soul has returned home to the spiritual side of reality.

Finally, I end with a loving and time-honoured tribute to my dear friend Jonathan Cainer. Thank you for being my Earth guide, and for providing inspiration. You will be deeply missed divine friend. God speed on your evolutionary and spiritual ascension through the spirit world, heaven has embraced a beautifully-polished and perfectly-faceted soul.

Thank you . . .

. . . To my father Robert Wheatcroft, for your continued support in the face of adversity. And for your love, kindness and your understanding. I am pleased you have finally seen the light.

To Ann Smallcorn, for your tender care, guidance, understanding and for your long-standing support and kindness. Thank you most graciously for the love you gave freely and unconditionally. A Heavenly Accolade awaits you in the spirit world dear heart. God bless!

To Pamela Oliver, for your spiritual love, friendship and guidance, and perhaps more importantly for the timely and divine correspondence you have freely expressed over the years. Also, for embracing the beautiful gift of astrology, I am delighted and overjoyed with your progress. May you spiritual progression reign eternal!

To my long-standing and a dear friend Geoff Mercer, for your important spiritual contribution to this publication, your spiritual insight, and perhaps more importantly for your priceless friendship. Long may it continue. Blessings!

To Laura Coramai, for your timely assistance with regards to your recommendation of Saltire Books. Also, thank you for your professional guidance and your moral support, it was greatly appreciated. God Bless!

To Dovid Strusiner, for your insightful inspiration, your heartfelt connection, your kindness, your professional support, and your spiritual guidance.

To Kathy Allan, for your input, your wisdom and the valuable insight purporting to the importance of the planetary rulers of the Nodes, from which an entire book was born hence: *One Body Many Illnesses, An Insightful Approach to Medical Astrology*. I am grateful.

To my good friend and editorial guide Paul F. Newman, for your expert suggestions and for your professional eye. All of my achievements would prove to be "incomplete" without your valuable input.

To Alice Miller, for helping me to attain further spiritual insight at the mid-life juncture that marks the second Saturn return.

To Donna Cunningham, for your timely assistance, your valuable input; and for our forged collaboration, that has been incredibly beneficial.

To David Spencer (loving known as Rej) for your love, your guidance and your wisdom. May God bless you on your evolutionary and eternal journey upon the physical and spiritual plane.

To Richard Smoot and all the staff at ISAR (International Society for Astrological Research) for your continued support and belief in me.

To Steven Kayne chief editor at Saltire Books, for your professional honesty and good wishes, and for endorsing my first major publication.

To Margaret Cahill, for your support and encouragement over the years. I hope your recovery back to improved health continues. Best wishes!

To Rachel Dalley, for your friendship and your kindly assistance, that allowed the continuation of this publication. Thank you!

To Oscar Cainer, for providing further inspirational guidance; and for continuing the invaluable and uplifting work that exhilarated your uncle Jonathan.

To NB, for providing the appropriate residence that spawned *One Body Many Illnesses*.

Lastly, to the spiritual teacher Louise L. Hay. Thank you for being a long-term source of inspiration and spiritual guidance. Long may it continue, love, light and blessings!

A Final Tribute . . .

. . . To Kris Brandt Riske, Jack Cipolla and all the staff at the AFA (American Federation of Astrologers), for believing I had something worthwhile to share and as a result publishing my first major publication: *One Body Many Illnesses, An Insightful Approach to Medical Astrology.*

Foreword

Everyone who has enjoyed Alan's previous book *One Body Many Illnesses* will be delighted I'm sure to read more in this further volume *Astrology for Self-Healing, The Essential Guide*.

The work this time covers many new ideas and examples in the meaning of astrological cycles and aspects and gives us Alan's view as to how these can be used and understood in the prognosis, treatment and prevention of various illnesses and diseases.

Paul F. Newman
Author of the excellent title: Luna (The Astrological Moon)

An Important Message from the Author

"The Akashic Record (Sanskrit word meaning 'sky', 'space' or 'ether') is a vital aid for spiritual research because ultimately it reveals the absolute truth."---Sneh Chakraburtty, Rtd, MD, writer of Women-Child Empowerment Projects

Someone once asked me "how can the planets in the solar system possible affect us?" This is a familiar question, and one that is often directed in a cynical capacity, mostly for the purpose of castigating astrology. Meanwhile, this is my answer:

An important part of evolution as an incarnated soul upon the Earth plane is to discern what this third planet from the Sun has to offer in terms of heightened experience. Originally, the Earth was a magnet for pristine harmony, and was known throughout this particular region of space for its crystalline structures and beautifully defined vistas.[1] But that was many millions of years ago when the Earth was projected and perceived as a jewel-like sphere emanating celestial potential. As souls we originally visited the Earth to experience certain aspects of physicality. Similarly, the other planets in the solar system were also projected as jewel-like spheres of infinite magnitude and potential.[2]

Currently, the Earth, caught in a concretized and twisted state of dark polluted confinement and dis-ease, magnifies and projects apathy and materialism. Apathy is a construct for illness, disease and violence, whereas extreme materialism is an adornment for greed and corruption. A wise man once said: "the material world is full of roads with dead ends."[3] Likewise, the facets of greed, corruption, violence, illness and disease symbolize man-made fabrications for societal and planetary-wide collapse. Unfortunately, a systematic breakdown in global infrastructure is what's occurring now.

When the distant planets that form the backdrop of the cosmos affect us via transit, especially when they conjunct a personal planet or an angle such as the Ascendant in the natal chart, the planet's electromagnetic energy impacts on us in a way that appears as if we are being pressed subconsciously into visiting those transiting spheres of influence in order to experience a certain set of circumstances pertaining to self-healing.

Thus, the traditional and metaphysical experiences orchestrated by transiting planets are mostly for the purpose of augmenting the soul's karma and facilitating spiritual progression (the cornerstones for self-healing). This becomes particularly relevant when Saturn, Uranus and Neptune are involved.

In addition, the astrological degree that each natal planet occupies represents a pressure point in the natal chart. During periods when natal planets are activated (via transits) these pressure points are perceived as either vulnerable or receptive. In most cases, pressure points are perceived as vulnerable when they are influenced by frictional squares and oppositions, and are perceived as receptive when they are influenced by conjunctions and the much softer trines. How we perceive these points and the potential that can be achieved from them depends solely on the level of spiritual progression the soul has attained.

Every human being that frequents the plane of the Earth has incarnated with the cosmos circumscribing their physical persona. Many are simply unaware, whereas many are in complete denial. This is why astrology is frequently dismissed as abstract and hypothetical.[4] The key to understanding astrology is to raise the soul's vibration; and with the assistance of the aforementioned planets, astrology helps us to remember our spiritual heritage. Elevating the soul's vibration is the ultimate purpose of incarnation.

Finally, and to quote the Akashic Records, I will draw this section to conclusion by simply saying: Astrology is a physical and spiritual discipline that represents the Absolute Truth. If we understood what astrology truly symbolized there would be no need for self-healing.

Proof that Astrology Actually Works

In a recent study published in the Spanish journal *Medicina Clinica*, Spanish scientists ascertained that "your chronic health issues may be written in the stars."[5] They concluded that at least some forms of astrology are not nonsense after all by discovering a link between the month of birth and future chronic health problems. The study is the latest to show that the conditions, especially during pregnancy and the first year of life, can have an effect that persists through mature adulthood.

Scientists have now discovered that Pisces people are more intuitive, Geminis are quick-witted, and Sagittarians are philosophical and empathetic. And for Virgos? Well they have a statistically significant increased risk of thyroid problems and asthma.

Almost 30,000 patients were involved in the research, in which scientists from the University of Alicante mapped people's month of birth on to 27 different health problems ranging from incontinence to migraine. The study found that men born in June and December had the highest risk of developing osteoarthritis, while those born in April had the lowest risk of developing back problems.

In women, the researchers found that eight conditions seemed to have a link to the month of birth. These included incontinence, which was the highest in June babies, and high cholesterol, which was worse in those born in October.

They concluded that the month of birth may behave as an indicator of periods of early exposure to various factors, such as exposure to ultraviolet rays, temperature, seasonal exposure to viruses and allergies etc, which may affect the development of the uterus and neonate in the first months of life. High doses of vitamin D were recommended as prevention in all cases.

And all of this was based merely on the month of birth under the rulership of the specific zodiac sign. It is clear that as mankind envelops the energies of the approaching Age of Aquarius, attitudes are beginning to alter significantly, as fear of the unknown is purged.

Endnotes

[1] The Earth is not the static home many of us believe it to be. The illusion of physicality has occurred because a large percentage of souls have turned away from God and have therefore lost sight of their spiritual heritage; and so many are simply unaware of this. This unfortunate fact is due to a cataclysm that occurred millions of years ago from which we are all still feeling the effects. There are many references and information available citing this catastrophic occurrence.

[2] Frictional aspects such as squares, quincunxes and oppositions are often adverse because the planets throughout the solar system are only projecting a fraction of their potential due to their current distorted and polluted form. All the planets are meant to be crystalline spheres of infinite potential.

[3] Reference to the Indian spiritual teacher Prem Rawat.

[4] With this reference I ask you to consider the fact that the planets were also affected by the cataclysm muddying our perception of astrology even more.

[5] An article that appeared in *The Times* newspaper on the 21st June 2017, aptly on the summer solstice.

Welcome to the Age of Aquarius
(The New Kingdom of Light)

Consecrated Messages of Hope

At the dawning of the Age of Pisces a single Christed body elected to reincarnate on Earth in order to raise awareness—towards the approaching epoch. That was the soul of the much-publicized spiritual master and teacher Jesus Christ. In ancient Hebrew, Jesus means *Salvation*; and the journey towards salvation is associated with the sign of Pisces and its ancient ruler Jupiter. In the scriptures contained in the Modern Hebrew bible Jesus translates as Yeshua, and Yeshua in Hebrew derives from the verbal translation hence 'to rescue' (Neptune the modern ruler of Pisces), and also "to deliver" (Mercury the polarity planet of Jupiter).[1]

As Jesus made his evolutionary journey he inspired the souls of his worshipers, who in return helped him to extend his message of wisdom (Jupiter). Jesus offered the path to salvation (Jupiter and Pisces) to anyone who wished to reclaim their spiritual heritage, comprised of the wisdom of his knowledge (Mercury, Jupiter and Neptune). These worshipers became known as the disciples, followers of God—Jupiter (representing the almighty saviour in esoteric astrology); and Neptune and Pisces (translating as the soul of God and man the disciple).

At that time Jupiter, meaning the celestial body of wisdom in ancient mythology, was designated as the ruler of Pisces, as Neptune, the modern-day ruler of Pisces, hadn't yet been discovered. The fact that Neptune had not yet been discovered was partly why so many at that time remained unconvinced that Christ was a highly-evolved (Christed) soul, hence the son of God that he is now more commonly referred to. The dense fog emanating from an undiscovered Neptune was clearly evident at that time in a period of tremendous discord and defiance. However, the purpose of the Piscean Age was to remind humankind that we are all children of the Creator.

Christ incarnated in order to lift the fog of despair so that those who wished to embrace his message could begin to see their way with a renewed clarity of vision.

A Group Collective

Today, as humankind sits at the threshold of the new age, the Age of Aquarius, not one but a group collective of highly-evolved souls representing a wave of prodigious intellect (Aquarius), have elected to return to physicality in order to raise awareness towards the approaching epoch. These souls have and are continuing to incarnate at different points upon the plane of the Earth, and they are incarnating from a total of eight soul groups displaying higher-mindedness (eight is the number represented by Uranus in numerology). According to the Akashic Records this process culminated at the seventh and final square of Uranus and Pluto in 2015 (seven is Neptune's number in numerology).

Similar to the dangers and condemnation Christ encountered, these wise and divinely-mature souls (Saturn the traditional ruler of Aquarius) who have returned within the previous five Pluto generations (from Virgo through to Capricorn) are equally aware of the perils they face in a fragmented and disbelieving world. This group symbolize a prominent mark of colossal strength (Saturn). During Pluto's ingress of Capricorn these souls have and are continuing to work harder in order to instil awareness as Saturn demands that their wisdom must break though the concretized barriers of mankind's ignorance. Duly they will receive their spiritual rewards during Pluto's transit of Aquarius.[2]

Appropriately and collectively speaking, perhaps we should refer to these interconnected souls as The Oasis of Transformation, especially in honour of Pluto's forthcoming ingress into humanitarian Aquarius—transformation from the oasis of Pisces.

There are evolutionary markers in the natal charts of these

highly-evolved souls who are here voluntarily, as opposed to those being drawn back into incarnation due to the magnetic pull of the Earth, and temptation (refer to Chapter 3) and unfinished business, to seed the new age. Astrologically, these markers are referred to as Interceptions.[3] Or, as another well-known astrologer quite eloquently cites: Starseed or Starborn![4] We are all blessed!

The Definition of Aquarius

Spiritual awakening, sublime humanitarianism and political reform are the predominant and lasting themes of the new Aquarian Age. During the next seventy years as extremism increases, positive and effective cures will be found for the global illnesses of greed, violence and corruption. Never before has humankind experienced such a drastic and uncertain period of alternation within the natural course of evolution—that which was placed by Pisces will be purged by Aquarius.

From this point forward the political, social, and religious infrastructures of the world will change dramatically as the waters that flow from the almighty Aquarian Urn germinate seeds of self-realization, higher intuition and collective consciousness. The resonant vibrations of the Great Aquarian Passion Play will generate new levels of awareness and responsibility as Aquarian dialogues replace the distorted tones that continue to resonate from the broken instrument of Poseidon—narratives of illusion and deceit. Ultimately, the Piscean Fish will return to the depths of the cosmic ocean.[5]

The Age of Aquarius is the futuristic epoch associated with higher-mindedness and technological advancement; and for the sole purpose of liberation from the illusion of entrapment. I feel it is important that I reiterate this brief but important piece to coincide with The New Kingdom of Light. It was first published in my previous publication: One Body Many Illnesses:

Unfortunately, there are no solutions at the physical level to the problems that we continue to endure upon this planet. The answers will only transpire when we change our way of thinking. In order to save ourselves and our planet Earth from potential cataclysm before it is too late, we need to learn to think from the heart-mind as opposed to the head-mind. The issues of despair and degradation that are prevalent throughout the world are occurring because of the consequences created by the way in which we think. In essence, we have long 'forgotten' our spiritual heritage and therefore we have chosen to be disassociated from the divine consciousness.

Endnotes

[6] Information from *Wikipedia*.

[7] Information source the Akashic Records.

[8] An interception is a zodiac sign that has no house cusps. It is situated between a pair of houses either side.

[9] Reference to the Reverend Alice Miller.

[10] This short piece was originally compiled by the author in 2008 and subsequently published by Wander Sellar for the *Astrology and Medicine Newsletter* in the same year.

Preface

"Three things that cannot be hidden, the Sun, the Moon and the Truth."—The Buddha

Compiling this book has been a privilege. It has been written with guidance from the spiritual heart; and from the information retrieved from the Akashic Records.

First, and most important, I would like to say Thank You to the divine intelligence for inspiring me to compile this essential and timely publication at this karmic cyclical juncture — tightly woven within the evolutionary tapestry of humankind. A momentous and transformational epoch that initially began in 2012. As the winds of change gather strength and unrivalled direction, the vibration that represents the collective cosmic consciousness is preparing the way for the approaching Age of Aquarius for those who chose to embrace its potential.[11]

Astrology for Self-Healing

Astrology for Self-Healing is NOT a book for the beginner. Nor has it been specifically compiled for the professional astrologer. Rather, it is a book for those who wish to expand their knowledge via a deeper and more intrinsic level of astrological understanding.

Packed full of elemental and startling insights that have become overlooked in a fragmented world where the future remains uncertain, this publication details the supportive and spiritual interplay housed in the dynamics of the astrological natal chart—representative of our physical, psychological and spiritual bodies. The natal chart is a projection of the soul's strengths, weaknesses and karmic purpose and can be described as both a unique universal blue print and a cosmic compass to pointing out the potential for soul healing and evolutionary transformation.

Despite the misgivings expressed by modern-day religions and popular scientists as to its rationale and legitimacy—incorrectly labelling astrology as a pseudo-science—its cosmic influence nevertheless manages to break through the barriers of tradition and ignorance to inspire, create and reveal the soul's potential, with purpose and enlightenment as the rewards.

At every point on the Earth sphere a profound vibration of change is now evident. The flawed ideologies and belief systems of humankind's distant past are beginning to break down, disintegrate and transmute. The Earth is once again encompassing divine light transmitted with love from the higher influences. The Earth plane is purging and realigning its core matrix with the divine to reclaim his spiritual heritage.[12]

This is partly why there is so much chaos, disorder and violence in societies today—atrocities committed by fallen souls who have chosen not to embody the LIGHT changes overseen, in part, by domiciled Neptune transiting Pisces. Unfortunately, many souls prefer to remain concealed in the dark illusion cast by a perishing fragmentation that was once a powerful image of hope—the once gloriously-proposed Age of Pisces (the Christ epoch).

Synergizing with these changes are the planets in the cosmos. With the recent square configurations between Uranus (planet of astrology) and Pluto (transformation) astrology has and is continuing a powerful rebirth that is impacting on so many more souls across the world. Astrology continues to inspire individual souls, spiritual groups and esoteric movements, with one common aim: to transcend towards the supernal light of hope and remembrance of who we are. These are all noticeable signs of the much-publicized Age of Aquarius (healing via the power of higher-mindedness).

Unlike the other eleven Great Ages on the cyclic sphere of evolution the potential of the Age of Aquarius is *quaquaversal*, meaning its energy has the potential to be propelled in every conceivable direction (via the physical, psychological and the spiritual bodies).

Across the globe, groups of like-minded souls are gathering with one aim in mind, to pour light into the Earth and to transcend the negative vibrations enveloping many of its degenerate civilizations. Currently, these light gatherings are ever more widespread and noticeable as the bearers of love and light increase. Simply put, astrology is a universal language that can reveal the soul's chosen path as it traverses the plane of physicality. Astrology is also a valuable asset that is instrumental in the art of self-healing.

In order to heal we must first understand the actual nature of the perceived infirm (physical or psychological) that creates the imbalance. And what better way to discover that lifeline of hope, available to everyone who wishes to advance spiritually, than the time-honoured tradition of astrology. Astrology envelopes the energy and power of the cosmos for us to use as an asset for progression.

An Evolutionary Journey

Humankind has now arrived at a crucial evolutionary juncture where chaos and disorder are proliferating and threaten to annihilate its collective consciousness, or so it would seem. Yet all that is occurring today has happened before. Time and time again we have become trapped in a cyclic bubble of illusion, and now in order to survive we must raise our soul vibration. To cap it all the Earth has entered into an apparent state of flux abound with natural disasters. However, we have also entered into a period where only the truth can prevail.

In the meantime what can we all do to raise our vibration? We must look within the spiritual heart for answers via meditation and stillness, and remember who we are. We must promote unconditional love, and send it out to the collective consciousness of humankind and the planet. We should remain conscious and aware, and take great care of our physical bodies, because without the blessing of good health none of this can be successfully achieved. There are so many on the Earth who continue to damage their souls via appalling diets, alcohol consumption and drug abuse, primarily because of apathy, blinkeredness and ignorance. What's more, so many are simply unaware of the dangers and the side effects attached to abusing the body in this way.

Writing this publication has been no easy matter. It has taken many painstaking years of research. I have spent a good deal of time perusing the Akashic Records, which invariably leaves me with a feeling of euphoria, and I only hope that you, the reader, are inspired and enlightened by this achievement.

However, extracting information from the Akashic Records can also leave one feeling emotionally and mentally exhausted. Lapis lazuli (Mastery and Neptune) is an Earth element that aligns the crown chakra with the Akashic Records. The ancient Egyptian civilizations (circa Age of Taurus, 4000BC-1800 BC) knew this fact all too well. Evidentially they wore animal-shaped pieces of lapis that touched their skins representative of the signs of the zodiac. Lapis helps the body to recover from mental and physical exhaustion. Although work of this nature shouldn't be tiring, it is because the field of energy surrounding the Earth is set to negative that causes the body to leach its natural resources. This is partly why there is so much illness and disease today.

Also, writing this publication has allowed me to traverse further along my spiritual path; and my hope is that it assists those like-minded souls who also need to be further awakened and inspired by its healing messages. My hope is that it will raise awareness with those who express a keen interest in the discipline of astrology. Despite the frequent misgivings applied to this science, never before on our collective evolutionary journey has the healing potential of astrology been so desperately needed. Humankind now sits at a crucial pinnacle where the prospect of light-enhanced higher mindedness can be freely embraced;

and with that said, I would like to further acknowledge the approaching Age of Aquarius.

Alternatively, we can, if we choose, become further entrenched in the prospect of devastating destruction, already rife in our degenerate societies, and on a scale never witnessed in the last 10,000 years, be it natural or manmade. We can, if we choose, continue to promote ignorance and become engrossed by the darkness. As each day passes we witness ruination in almost every part of the world, with wars being threatened almost everywhere. However, it is never too late for positive change on any level—conscious change that will ultimately orchestrate self-healing and the necessary healing for our long-suffering planet. We simply have to choose the power of positive change.

My advice is: choose the light. As always the end result is reliant on the free choices of every individual! Embracing the supernal light will avert the prospect of cataclysm, which looms in the not too distant future.

I would like to turn my thoughts again briefly to the approaching Age of Aquarius, and to say: "Those souls who chose to return to the Earth plane in order to help raise awareness in view of this approaching epoch have done so consciously and lovingly." This book is also a testament to them. God bless you for your courage and inner strength!

Finally, I hope that as each chapter unfolds it will resonate in the spiritual heart as a vibration of remembrance, and as an elevated symbol of divine truth. Choose love as opposed to hate, and stay safe at this difficult time.

Blessings to you, the dear readers!
Alan Richards Wheatcroft

Endnotes

[1] The Irish astrologer Cyril Fagan (1896-1970) suggested that the vernal sidereal and tropical zodiacs coincided in 221AD and

hence the Age of Aquarius will not be truly with us until the 24th century. Like many astrologers I too resonate towards this hypothesis.

[2]According to the Akashic Records the Earth is predominantly male. Logically speaking this would surely have to be the case as its satellite the Moon is predominantly seen as female, thus producing a balanced vibrational polarity. Despite the opinions of popular scientists the Moon is *not* the Earth's natural satellite. Millennia ago the Moon was placed within the Earth's gravitational field to symbolize the divide between male and female, which is very evident today.

Astrology: A Universal Language

Astrology is the study of synthetic patterns, connections and polarities.—Nancy B. Detweiler

Zodiacal and planetary influences—elemental foundation points of the natal chart—have been spiritually integrated into the aura (the chakral and biorhythmic energy field), as a source of creativity, challenge and potential. These are the cornerstones of infinite possibility. Likewise, astrology is a catalyst for the evolutionary transformation of a human soul, providing a vantage point from which the soul can observe its own destiny.

Interwoven with its modern, traditional, mundane and cultural roots, and perceived by the esoterically-minded as a quantum-based science, astrology is best described as a universal language. It is a cosmic compendium of potential, a limitless fountain of knowledge, comprising juxtaposing viewpoints, futuristic ideologies and heartfelt perspectives. Astrology symbolises a multi-dimensional and celestial cosmos.

The essence or soul of infinite possibility is exemplified by a continually-changing stream of cosmic vibrations, each resonating in colored tones at multiple frequencies. Every sign of the zodiac (metabolic condition), and planet (sphere of potential), that moves along a separate yet interconnected trajectory through the cosmos, represents a manifestation of polarised energy particles and projections. The cosmos exhibits dual purpose—until its energy coalesces to become a single unified force.

Astrology determines that the signs and planets provide a set of circumstances that will create multiple choices and karmic experiences that lead us to the realisation, and procurement of the divine plan (the purpose of physical incarnation). The celestial cosmos is a reflection, a projection and a delineation of the karma of the soul's internal compass—its route to salvation. In current technological terms it might be appropriate to say the soul's SATNAV: Satellite Navigation System.

If every human being understood these fundamental facts and projected his or her thoughts from the heart-mind there would be no apathy, greed, violence and no illness and disease on planet Earth. Choosing to ride the rollercoaster of incarnation and uncertainty, as opposed to progressing on the spiritual plane of serenity and bliss, would not be necessary.

Multiple souls continually reincarnating for the wrong reasons is a further example of why illness and disease has always existed; and worse proliferated.

Astrology: Changing Politics

"The collective principle asserts that…no society can legitimately call itself civilised if a sick person is denied medical aid because of a lack of means."—Aneurin Bevan MP, from his book: *In Place of Fear*, page 100.[1]

I begin my deliberations with a succession of interviews given throughout the course of 2015 by the British conservative MP David Tredinnick.[2] In his first interview, he told the *Daily Mail* newspaper group that: "astrology had a proven track record especially when it comes to helping people recover from illness and should be incorporated into standard medical treatments." He went on to say, "I am absolutely convinced that those who look at the map of the sky for the day that they were born and receive some professional guidance will find out a lot about themselves and it will make their lives easier."

In a second interview to the *Daily Mail* he said: "astrology is something that people should be aware of as an option they have if they are confused about themselves and should not be attacked when it has a proven track record." During the same interview he also revealed that Chris Patten, Britain's last governor to Hong Kong, had an official astrologer.

In a further interview to *The Times* newspaper group he said: "waiting times with the National Health Service (NHS) could be significantly reduced if doctors looked at the cosmos in order to highlight a patient's susceptibility to certain conditions." During the same interview Mr Tredinnick branded critics of astrology, such as Professor Brian Cox as "racially prejudiced especially when they have never studied the subject." The criticism came to light when Brian Cox's exceptionally-produced scientific documentary: *Wonders of the Cosmos*, was first being shown on British television. During one episode Professor Brian Cox remarked that "astrology was a load of rubbish." Consequently, this sparked a retributive response throughout the astrological community, especially in the UK, when some astrologers branded Mr Cox as a bigot. The MP for Bosworth and Leicestershire in the United Kingdom is also a supporter of naturopathic homeopathy. He told *The Times* newspaper group during the same interview that he "believed opposition to astrology and assisted practices can be 'deeply offensive' to people especially in Asian communities who believe in such practices." He also pointed out that other politicians—from Ronald Reagan to Winston Churchill and the French general Charles de Gaulle—had subsequently made use of the stars.

In another interview, Mr Tedinnick told the Astrological Association of Great Britain that: "scientists who opposed the idea that the movement of celestial bodies can affect people's lives on Earth were being superstitious and ignorant, because they have never studied the subject and say that it is all to do with what appears in the newspapers, which it is not. They are deeply prejudiced, and racially prejudiced, which is troubling."

Finally, he told MPs in the House of Commons: "Ninety percent of pregnant French women use astrology as well as homeopathy. Astrology is a diagnostic tool enabling us to see strengths and weaknesses via the birth chart. Astrology was, until modern times, part of the tradition of medicine. I think it is a great pity that so many scientists today are dismissive of right-side brain energy, such as intuition. Unfortunately, organizations such as the BBC (British Broadcasting Corporation) are quite dismissive of astrology and seek to promote the science perspective and always seem keen to broadcast criticisms. The opposition of astrology is based on what I call the SIP formula—superstition, ignorance and prejudice."

Endnotes

[1] Aneurin (Nye) Bevan MP was the founder of the National Health Service (NHS) in the UK in 1948. It was reported after his death that he frequently showed a keen interest in astrology.

[2] David Tredinnick is regarded as one of the UK's outspoken and

controversial politicians who has helped fellow MPs with life changing decisions. He famously said in a speech in the House of Commons: "Consulting the stars would take huge pressures off doctors, and [he predicted that] astrology will have a role to play in future healthcare." He is also a member of two influential Commons committees, the health and science and technology committees. He is also vice chairman of the government's herbal medicines working group.

xxx

Part One
Preliminaries

"Humankind is born with two incurable *diseases*,
life from which it inevitably dies, and hope which
hints that death may not be the end."
—Andrew Greeley[1]

Chapter One

An Ancient Belief System

"He who practices medicine without the benefit of the movement of the stars and the planets is not a doctor but a fool."— Hippocrates

The famous herbalist and physician Nicholas Culpeper (1616-1654) used the techniques of astrology alongside his herbal medicines. The decumbiture chart would be used for the diagnosis and Culpeper would treat the illness appropriately. He is often quoted as saying: "Only astrologers are fit to study medicine and a physician without astrology is like a lamp without oil." (Refer to Chapter 10, The Importance of Herbs, Vitamins and Minerals in the Natal Chart, for in-depth analyses about Nicholas Culpeper.)

This initial chapter represents an in-depth extension of the material presented as the opening chapter in my previous publication *One Body Many illnesses, An Insightful Approach to Medical Astrology* (see Additional Publications at the end of this book). Now, and with the inclusion of some timely additions, it continues to serve as a reminder that *healing* is paramount at every level of evolutionary progression—referring to the physical, psychological and spiritual bodies of consciousness. If you are unfamiliar with my previous publication, I hope you find the information here insightful and perhaps beneficial.

An Introduction to Medical Astrology

Medical astrology is an ancient system of interpretation that associates with the many diverse and intricate parts of the body, both externally and internally; and the unfortunate implications that can endure as a result of illness and disease. Medical astrology shows the potential for illness and disease in the natal chart and confirms the diagnosis of the infirm, especially during periods of frictional transits. To start the prognosis a decumbiture chart (a medical horary chart) is used. Decumbiture chart diagnosis is preferred by some medical astrologers as an alternative to natal chart diagnosis.

The potential for illness and disease and for healing is listed under the rulership of the Sun, the Moon and the planets. In some cases healing is successfully implemented via spiritual meditations; this of course is dependent on the individual's preference and relevant belief system. In most cases however, healing comes through conventional means, such as prescribed medicines, and alternatively through holistic-based remedies, such as homeopathy—both of which alleviate the symptoms and bring about a resolution by assisting the body's natural process of healing.

The planets and their interconnected aspects, the twelve astrological signs, and the qualities of the signs, i.e. the cardinal, the fixed and the mutable, highlight the potential effects further, and also the possible outcome of the disease. On occasion, it is possible to determine an illness or disease as terminal.

Mutable Quality Signs

If the qualities of the signs are being influenced by frictional planetary aspects such as squares, quincunxes and oppositions and particularly by semi-sextiles,[2] the mutable signs (Gemini, Sagittarius, Virgo and Pisces) show the potential for diseases such as tuberculosis, and specific mental type illnesses such as psychosis, schizophrenia, and particularly dementia. The sign qualities coupled with the signs of the zodiac are essentially filters or enhancers for the planet's vibrational energies. This can be noted as filters for the soft aspects and enhancers for the hard aspects.

Currently, many western civilizations are beset by what can only be described as a health bomb, a proliferating and impending explosive contagion called dementia. Thus, dementia can be likened to an indefinable prolific echo; an abstract reverberation of a concerning health problem that most likely occurred earlier in life. In most cases, dementia occurs as a consequence of long-term depression and the dis-ease known today as bipolar disorder, which are dis-eases categorized under the rulership of Saturn. Therefore, we can ascertain that dementia is a condition that also falls under the influence of Saturn.

Physiologically, dementia occurs because the mindset constantly replays a recurring theme, which in many cases configures something like this: "it wasn't like this in my day," and "why should I change." This is why dementia is primarily associated with elderly people, paying particular attention to the Pluto in Cancer generation—souls who are inclined to obsess over their long-term memories. These latent images have become augmented by pleasurable familiarities, and/or entrenched in life grudges and emotional grievances. In my estimation these statistics accrue to 70 percent of souls from this particular Pluto-influenced group. Obsessing over the long-term memory can cause fragmentation and deterioration to the short-term memory.

A high percentage of spiritual astrologers, including myself, believe the Moon has rulership over the short-term memory, and therefore manipulates the hippocampus; the neurological center that dementia ultimately affects. For further information about the Moon's rulership over the short-term memory see Chapter 8, Evolutionary Memory.

Fixed Quality Signs

The fixed signs (Taurus, Scorpio, Leo and Aquarius), when influenced by hard aspects such as oppositions, quincunxes, squares and particularly by semi-squares, highlight the potential for heart conditions such as cardiovascular disease and cardiomyopathy. Fixed signs also have a tendency for strokes (CVA – Cardio Vascular Accident). Furthermore, the fixed signs highlight the potential for specific types of cancer, such as bowel, throat and lymph node cancer.

Cardinal Quality Signs

The cardinal signs (Aries, Cancer, Libra and Capricorn), when under the influence of hard aspects such as oppositions, quindeciles, quincunxes and squares, highlight the potential for tumours, both benign and malign, and particularly tumours that form in the brain, breasts, kidneys, and liver. Often tumours turn out to be benign when trines are located in the chart influencing the cardinal signs. Also, the cardinal signs have a potential for kidney dis-eases such as kidney stones and bone degenerative diseases such as osteoporosis.

Illness Preordained

According to our ancient spiritual ancestors (circa pre-Atlantis) who widely practiced this now-forgotten discipline, a planet posited in a particular sign can indicate a weakness in the sign's energy field, so that when the planet is subject to certain conditions, the combination of planetary and zodiac energies can manifest as injury, illness and even fatality. The effects largely depend on the karmic quality of the aspects between the planets in the natal chart, and the strength of the transitory cycles that occur throughout the natural course of life.

There are many, including myself, who believe that illness is preordained (because everything you are experiencing now has happened before in past incarnations). So for most souls, physicality is a cycle of cause and effect. Reoccurring illness is dependent on the type of karma bestowed upon the soul, and the levels of awareness the soul has attained previously (more about understanding consciousness in Chapter 4, The Counterpoint

Effect). The information with reference to our ancient ancestors was successfully retrieved from the Akashic Records.

In most cases, illness and disease are considered merely as by-products that emanate from the choices made by the individual via the application of free will—negative constructs of the head mind. If the lifestyle was fraught with a heavy consumption of alcohol and hard drugs like heroin and cocaine, it would be safe to assume that at some point on the life path the individual would suffer from liver, kidney or heart problems, possibly a combination of all three. This is all correct; however those choices that caused the alcohol and drug abuse happened before. Illusionary components such as dangerous substances are merely catalysts to exacerbate the karma (Saturn and Neptune).

Relevant to this is the modern cell phone obsession—obsessive tendencies that highlight the multiple use of cell phones. This disturbing problem is exacerbating. According to the World Health Organisation the over-usage of cell phones causes abnormalities in the brain such as the formation of malignant tumours. In addition, cell phone overuse causes cancer in specific parts of the brain such as the frontal lobe. Personally, I have found that most cell phone abuse is committed by those deemed the lost generation of the modern era (those souls born during the Uranus and Neptune transits of Aquarius: Uranus, circa 1996-2003, and Neptune, circa 1998-2012).

Medical Indications

The primary function of medical astrology is to provide the relevant indications as to whether the cosmic influences extant at the time of an illness are likely to be advantageous or disadvantageous to the individual. Therefore, as indicated in my previous publication, medical astrology functions on four essential points:
- The likely severity of the particular disease.
- The likely duration of the disease.

- The eventual and probable outcome of the disease.
- Any additional means that might be employed by a physician to counteract the disease and thus facilitate the restoration of the patient's health.

Further, the potential onset of illness and disease can be ascertained simply by examining the movements of the planets in the natal chart using the following astrological litany as a prospective guide, in which case caution and care concerning the health is strongly advised:

The first point is that illness and disease can manifest in the body when planets receive hard aspects to each other, especially when the planets form patterns such as T-squares, grand crosses, kites and yods. The main catalysts for illness and disease are: the 45-degree semi-square and the 90-degree square, the 150-degree quincunx and the 165-degree quindecile, and finally the 180-degree opposition. Pay particular attention to the square and the quincunx.

The second point is when afflicted planets and Nodal points such as: Mars, Saturn, North Node, South Node, Uranus, Neptune and Pluto tenant difficult houses such as the sixth, representing the place of the disease, the eighth house, representing the place of longevity, and the twelfth house, representing the place of death, the onset of illness and disease becomes a strong possibility. Alternatively, if these planets and points occupy Virgo, Scorpio and Pisces and receive hard aspects to each other, or to personal planets and the luminaries, illness and disease can also occur.

The third point is when all the planets listed above aspect the Ascendant, paying particular attention to the square and opposition. The Ascendant must always be considered in diagnosis because it symbolizes the mental body (mind), the physical body (anatomy) and the spiritual body (soul).

And finally, death is a relevant possibility when the Sun, Moon and Ascendant are aspected by any of the planets—especially when the Ascendant and the luminaries are afflicted simultaneously. Jupiter, Neptune and Pluto aspects must also be a consideration.

A further important point to remember is that illness and disease will only become a reality if we choose to live our lives in a constant negative mode. Meaning that we choose to neglect the physical body, feeding it poor quality nutrition and depleting the psychological profile of energy with negative thoughts. Our spiritual heart suffers because of a limited understanding and awareness to its very existence; and this notion exists because we do for the most part choose to ignore our spiritual roots.

Additional Causes

Moving on further, there are in medical astrology eleven similar classifications symbolizing illness and disease in addition to the four essential points listed above. These particular groupings form the basis for every known illness and disease, past and present. They are as follows:

- Neglect and deprivation (Saturn, Neptune).
- Congestion and blockage of energy release (Mars, Saturn, Neptune).
- Trauma and stress (Saturn, Uranus, North Node).
- Chemical, metal, and environmental toxins (Mars, Neptune, Pluto.
- Infection and contamination (Mars, South Node, Neptune).
- Parasites (Mars, Neptune, Saturn, North Node).

- Bites and stings leading to allergic reactions (Mars, Neptune, North Node, South Node).
- Physical and brain impairment leading to physical and mental deformity, etc. (Mars, Uranus, Pluto).
- Miasma and the residue of childhood diseases (Saturn, Neptune, Pluto).
- Psychological imbalance caused by the nature-nurture effect (Saturn, North Node, South Node, Uranus).
- Karmic imbalance (highlighting all categories) (Mars, Saturn, North Node, South Node, Uranus, Neptune, Pluto).

Here is a cross section of illnesses, diseases, conditions and impairments further influenced by the planets and Nodal points. This listing represents some of the most common aliments, mishaps and injuries prevalent throughout the world today:

- An afflicted Mars is the catalyst for burns, fevers, accidents, electric shocks, wounds caused by knives and other sharp implements, and implies suicidal tendencies and various types of cancer (particularly when Mars tenants Scorpio). A common example of an afflicted Mars can often lead to the onset of the Epstein-Barr virus, more commonly referred to as glandular fever.
- An afflicted Saturn is the catalyst for rheumatism, arthritis, asthma, and tuberculosis, deep-set depression and immune system malfunction such as organ failure. Also, Saturn can be the catalyst for lingering chronic illness and disease such as pancreatitis, with the inclusion of Parkinson's disease (indicating slowness of movement).
- An afflicted North Node is the catalyst for virtually every type of cancer known to mankind, except lymphoma, which includes Hodgkin's lymphoma (HL) and non-Hodgkin's lymphoma (NHL). These are caused primarily by afflictions from Mars, Jupiter, and Saturn.[3] A friend of mine developed bowel cancer at the time when the transiting North Node conjoined Saturn and squared Pluto in his

natal chart. An afflicted North Node, at the worse scenario, is the catalyst for leprosy (on the increase again), spleen diseases, pancreatic diseases and organ failure.
- An afflicted South Node is the catalyst for infectious diseases that have no known cure. Also, when transiting a planet such as Uranus, the South Node can be responsible for the onset of a complete mental breakdown. South Node diagnosis is similar to that of hazy Neptune in that it orchestrates the misdiagnosis of illness and disease—particularly if it has been a feature of a previous incarnation. This is because technically, previous incarnations are nothing but "mere illusions" that can no longer be related to. It should never be ruled out that the North and South Nodes are designated as exceptionally powerful points in medical astrology.
- An afflicted Uranus is the catalyst for heart attacks, electric shocks, gunshot wounds, brain diseases and tumours (often fatal). Also, it can be responsible for the malfunction and damage to the spinal chord, motor neurone disease, and causes arteries to block thus becoming diseased. Alongside Saturn and Pluto an afflicted Uranus is often the catalyst for Parkinson's disease and also Huntington's disease.[4]
- An afflicted Neptune is the catalyst for epilepsy, food poisoning, lunacy, drug and alcohol related diseases, drowning, and highly contagious diseases (often fatal) such as Ebola, and infectious viral diseases such as measles, chicken pox and scarlet fever. In some cases infectious viral diseases can lead to serious and life-threatening complications. These can include infections of the lungs such as pneumonia, and brain encephalitis, which are often misdiagnosed in mainstream diagnosis.
- Finally, an afflicted Pluto is the catalyst for syphilis, venereal diseases, HIV/AIDS, Epstein-Barr virus,[5] congenital diseases, Huntington's chorea, radiation poisoning and skin cancer due to overexposure to harmful UV and radioactive

rays. An afflicted Pluto is often wholly responsible for the deleterious side-effects associated with chemotherapy, radiation therapy and targeted therapy treatments.

Bringing this chapter about the important factors of medical astrology to a resolution are three sections concerning retrogrades, and the meaning given to Rx Zones and planetary reflections, and their likely connection to illness and disease:

Retrogrades

Before I proceed I thought it befitting to include a short verse on retrograde planets penned by my lifetime friend Anna Christy. "When planets go into reverse the message they convey is often one that helps us fight another day. They give us strength to make our own way and face up to the foe, to turn our feet and travel the other path, to leave behind the things that have troubled us in the past and to wipe clean the slate of life, at last.[6]

Planets (particularly Saturn) in retrograde motion represent a deeper awareness of the innate karmic signature typified by the planetary interplay of the natal chart.

Likewise, when an illness or a disease is identified in the natal chart and further diagnosed via a decumbiture chart,[7] both natal and transiting planets that appear in retrograde motion, paying particular attention to Saturn, Uranus, Neptune and Pluto, give rise to the notion that the infirm is congenital.

When planets are posited in signs in which they are in essential dignity or exalted they present heightened influence in the chart (see index of dignities at the end of the chapter). In most cases, when dignified and exalted planets station direct and begin gradual forward momentum they attain maximum impetus much quicker than when they are posited in the opposing signs—namely those signs considered their detriment or fall. This also applies when they are unaffected by any of these formidable dignities.

In the natal and decumbiture chart, planets in essential dignity or exaltation that are gathering pace from the effects of retrogradation, better assist the body's healing process. This is one reason why planets in essential dignity and exaltation are considered as proficient and freely display their energies more consistently.

Planets that are in detriment or in their fall, which are also gathering momentum from the effects of retrogradation, hinder the body's natural healing process (for more information see index of dignities at the end of this chapter). Planets in detriment create impasses that pose as challenging. Dignities are frequently overlooked. Many do not consider dignities to be important influences in modern astrology, but I would always recommend their use, especially in the practice of medical astrology.

Rx Zones

Rx Zones (planets that are in shadow) is a title given to planets entering into the cycle known as retrogradation. Before a planet is considered to be at its retrograde station it will begin a process of gradual deceleration, which can last for a couple of weeks in the case of Mercury and several months in the case of Pluto. Once a planet is at its direct station, ready to restart its forward momentum, it will have returned to the point it began its retrograde cycle. It is then that the planet leaves the Rx Zone and continues its trajectory around the Sun, and through its designated zodiac sign.

The length of time that planets move through the Rx Zone, which are points on the apparent trajectory as seen from Earth, it can, in most cases, be further detrimental to the health of an individual. That is providing of course that an illness or disease has been diagnosed—paying particular attention to mental health conditions. Zoned slow moving planets can also be the cause of mental illness, and planets in the Rx Zones can, in effect, add salt to the wound of the infirm, especially when these planets are aspected to the planets considered to be responsible for a particular condition. In addition, planets in the Rx Zone can hinder the healing process if Mars, Saturn, Uranus, Neptune and Pluto are strongly emphasized. Planets in Rx Zones are, in most cases, what slow down or interfere with the healing process.

Drawing upon my life experience of critical situations, when diseases such as cancer go into remission, it provides the individual with adequate time to orchestrate necessary and life-altering changes. It is often at the point when specific planets enter the Rx Zone that the illness is triggered into manifestation again. I have noticed on many an occasion that cancer and other illnesses recur when little or no change is implemented on the life path. Nor is the concept of change considered as a major necessity towards assisting the body with its healing process. In effect, for many, it is simply business as usual.

Finally, in my humble opinion, I consider that retrograde planets are given little or no consideration at all in medical astrology, even though they have a powerful and significant influence on the outcome of any illness or disease. The effects of retrogrades were covered briefly in my previous publication *One Body Many Illnesses*.

Planetary Reflections

When transitory aspects form and parallel or imitate those same aspects in the natal chart they become known as planetary reflections. So for example, if Venus makes an opposition to Pluto; and this aspect features in the natal chart, even if it is not joined to it in any way, the transit will have some influential bearing upon the individual concerned. In most cases however transiting aspects will be joined to natal aspects by minor aspectual influences, meaning they might sextile, square or trine them etc.

Nevertheless, when a planetary reflection parallels the natal aspect similar thoughts, feelings and actions that are determined by the natal aspect will surface and thus they will come to the forefront again, especially when one or more of the transiting planets are retrograde.

But let us return briefly to the Venus-Pluto opposition example and its effects. The financial pressures that may have tainted a personal or business relationship—those bones of contention that are concealed or ignored—will surface again causing further confrontation. Thus, this transit will inevitably mirror all the problems that this natal aspect stands for, and which are most likely obscured deep in the chart.

Equally, though, a Venus-Pluto opposition (natal or reflection) can provide additional depth and understanding to any relationship, depending on the strength of the personal connection in the first place. Planetary reflections often play out in a similar way to the situations highlighted in the 1990s movie *Groundhog Day* starring Bill Murray. The film depicted a self-centered individual trapped in a mire of recurring situations that ultimately re-enacted his worst nightmares that further highlighted his sublime ego.

The only way he could break free from this causality cycle was to transform his self-centered tendencies into expressive creativity and more importantly into compassion for those lesser mortals he considered others to be—well and truly beneath the limited confines of his own ego. Eventually he executed these transformational attributes magnificently. This film denoted beautifully the underlying problems that, in my opinion, all too frequently become a reflection of the opposition aspect.

To overcome the negative boundaries posed by an opposition a positive and balanced transformation in the psychological profile represented by those planets is all that is required. In other words to find the common ground that both parties can agree on. This concept equally applies to the square aspect. Planetary reflections provide us with this type of opportunity whether the aspect is a square, trine, quincunx or opposition. Simply put, when planetary reflections occur it is time to overcome the parameters we have set ourselves in its natal counterpart.

Planetary reflections that denote the soft aspects (trine, sextile etc) provide a chance to enhance our creative side; and to seize an opportunity that may have passed us by previously. This also applies to the special aspects: vigintile, decile, quintile etc.

Equally, planetary reflections can be a mirror for illness and disease, especially if the natal aspect that is in reflection was diagnosed as the primary cause of a specific condition. During these periods an individual is likely to reflect upon the illness once again; and in some cases a re-occurrence can occur simply by "willing it." For the most part, planetary reflections are a mirror image of a contracted, or a congenital illness or disease.

When under the influence of a planetary reflection, it is likely that diseases such as cancer that were previously in remission will return at some point, especially when the planetary reflection reaches the exact degree of the aspect that features in the natal chart. The effects of planetary reflections are similar to the effects of planets in shadow (Rx zones).

Personal Planetary Transits

Reoccurring personal planetary transits that are frictional in nature, such as squares, quincunxes and oppositions, are ongoing throughout the course of a lifetime (especially those that occur to the planetary rulers of the Sun sign and Ascendant) can eventually be overcome. In most cases, personal planetary transits, such as a Mars square to Saturn, are simply a source of emotional annoyance. But if evolutionary progression remains a priority throughout the course of incarnation the energy posed by personal planetary transits can be successfully transmuted.

Personal planetary transits act as projectors for illness and disease. They allow us to reflect on how we have progressed from a traumatic illness or disease. Alternatively, the frequent occurrence of personal planetary transits in the natal chart can be seen as negative disconcertions for the enhancement and the continuation of an illness or disease.

Final Conclusion

In my humble opinion, there is inadequate information available today, and virtually no observation given, to these pivotal facets of astrology, namely retrogrades and planetary reflections. Retrogrades are particularly significant because they represent important milestones reached mostly by reflective conjecture. Ancient civilizations recognized retrogrades and reflections as important pivotal influences. In order to alleviate the negative effects of planets in Rx Zones and planetary reflections I offer some practical and common sense advice:

Advice on Healing the Spiritual Body (Soul): I would advise regular exercises such as breath meditation, streamlined with the frequent use of visualization and color therapy if possible, in order to successfully heal the core of this infinite body.

Advice on Healing the Physical and Mental Body's (Life Force Energy): I would recommend a purely organic diet. This coupled with a sustainable meat and animal saturated fat,[8] yeast, sugar and gluten free plan, as the only suitable and commonsense approach to healing the life force.

Consistency in both examples would successfully prevent the onset of illness and disease—congenital or otherwise. A more detailed analysis of this advice can be found in Chapter 12, Guided Meditations, Healing the Mind, Body and Soul.

Planetary Dignities

Essential Dignity	*Detrimentation*
Sun in Leo	Sun in Aquarius
Moon in Cancer	Moon in Capricorn
Mercury in Gemini	Mercury in Sagittarius
Venus in Taurus	Venus in Scorpio
Venus in Libra	Venus in Aries
Mars in Aries	Mars in Libra

Jupiter in Sagittarius	Jupiter in Gemini
Saturn in Capricorn	Saturn in Cancer
Uranus in Aquarius	Uranus in Leo
Neptune in Pisces	Neptune in Virgo
Pluto in Scorpio	Pluto in Taurus

Exaltation	*Fall*
Sun in Aries	Sun in Libra
Moon in Taurus	Moon in Scorpio
Mercury in Virgo	Mercury in Pisces
Venus in Pisces	Venus in Virgo
Mars in Capricorn	Mars in Cancer
Jupiter in Cancer	Jupiter in Capricorn
Saturn in Libra	Saturn in Aries
Uranus in Scorpio	Uranus in Taurus
Neptune in Cancer	Neptune in Capricorn
Pluto in Aries	Pluto in Libra

Endnotes

[1] Andrew Greeley was a professor of sociology at the University of Chicago, 1954-1964.

[2] Semi-sextiles and quincunxes are aspects that are referred to as inconjuncts. These are aspects that culminate their orb of influence in disassociate signs, meaning they are either one sign (30 degrees) or five signs (150 degrees) apart from each other. They can be detrimental to health because their effects are deemed as inconsequential or at odds.

[3] Lymphoma is a group of blood cell tumours (Mars, blood, and Jupiter tumours) that develop from lymphocytes (a type of white blood cell). The name often refers to just the cancerous

ones rather than all such tumours. Signs and symptoms may include enlarged lymph nodes (Jupiter), fever (Mars), drenching sweats (Mars), weight loss and extreme fatigue (Mars, Saturn). However, the enlargements of lymph nodes are typically painless (Saturn).

[4]Huntington's disease (HD), also known as Huntington's chorea, is a genetic disease (Pluto) that results in death of brain cells (Mercury, Uranus), causing severe mental impairment and sudden jerky movements (Uranus). Parkinson's disease (PD) is a long-term disorder of the central nervous system that mainly affects the motor system (Uranus). These symptoms generally manifest slowly throughout time (Saturn). Most common symptoms are: shaking (Uranus), rigidity (Saturn), slowness of movement (Saturn) and difficulty walking (Mercury, Jupiter, Saturn).

[5]According to *Wikipedia* and The World Health Organisation (WHO) the Epstein-Barr virus (EBV), also called human herpesvirus 4 (HHV-4), is one of eight known viruses in the herpes family, and is one of the most common viruses to occur in humans. Infection with EBV occurs by the oral transfer of saliva, and genital secretions—typically Venus, *Mars*, Neptune and *Pluto* exploitations.

[6]Anna Christy is the author of *The Star Path* published in 1970 by Crucible Books.

[7]The decumbiture chart (also known as a medical horary chart), is normally cast at the time of diagnosis; and when the individual takes to their bed. Decumbiture charts are by far the most common approach to medical diagnosis in astrology used today.

[8]Natural saturated fat such as coconut and avocado oil is essential to the health of the body.

[9]According to some medical astrologers the body's white blood cells fall under the rulership of Saturn.

Chapter Two

Universal Law

> "Astrology, with all its diverse teachings, is the science that investigates the action and reaction constantly going on between the celestial bodies and the rest of manifested nature, thus revealing the laws under which this cosmic fusion takes place by way of the human condition."—Heinrich Daath

Without doubt this second chapter is one of the most significant of the entire book because it touches upon a precise few of the ancient spiritual truths. Unfortunately, in our modernistic 21st century world, we have all but chosen to misconceive, disbelieve and deny their very existence. These spiritual truths form part of the enlightened beliefs that the ancients referred to as Universal Law.

But in our present-day world, which is comprised mostly of total untruths, perhaps it would be more sagacious to rename these spiritual truths as the ones that contravene the concept of illness and disease.

Illness and Disease

Illness and disease symbolize imbalance within the psyche. Their impinging effects also project far-reaching consequences throughout the heart of humankind. The ruinous reverberations of illness and disease echo through the spirit world because many souls believe they are continually afflicted by an engrained condition long after the death of the physical body. This is especially relevant when dis-eases such as brain tumours, cancer and dementia are associated with death. The specific condition/conditions that caused the demise of the individual from the plane of physicality in the first place will remain as being terminal in the spirit world until the soul's perception is altered.

Also, there are a number of souls who believe that illness and disease are merely harbingers that exemplify the misconceptions surrounding the understanding of karmic law. This being the case, karmic law, as it is widely understood, has become disengaged from the truth; and truth is the symbolic representation of Universal Law.[1]

Karmic law represents the ultimate knowledge of soul expansion (Jupiter) and the attainment of ultimate spiritual wisdom (Saturn). Both of which expand the idea of spirituality—augmenting it further via the plane of physicality. Universal Law is a heavenly projection of the divine consciousness onto the plane of physicality by the spiritual masters: Jupiter, Saturn, Uranus, Neptune and Pluto.

Universal Law

Before I deliberate further, I would like to summarize this book with a spiritual certitude; and one that will hopefully reveal why these centuries-old misbeliefs are still at the forefront of modern existence. It is a principle attached solely to the divine context of Universal Law, and is a numinous message that is delivered directly from the heart of the Akashic Records. It appears in a similar format throughout many of the Ancient Tibetan Wisdom Teachings—beautifully outlined throughout much of Alice A. Bailey and Alan Oken's soul-centered work.[2]

It is a powerful maxim that relays a straightforward message; the key principle of Universal Law:

Universal Law determines that if a human being is to avoid the unpleasantness associated with illness and disease he or she must instinctively learn to raise the heart's vibration and think solely from the mind of the heart, as opposed solely to the mind of the head. Moreover, he or she must re-familiarize with the innate power and value of divine faith. Ultimately, as spiritual beings on a human journey, we are not meant to experience the trappings of illness or disease.

Forgotten Astrological Wisdom

So, dear reader, if your heart resonates with the delightful melodies and coloured vibrations and textures of light energy that are associated with the heart-mind as a result of heightened awareness, you will naturally understand this enlightening message. Also, if you live your life in continual remembrance of the heart-mind, where you embrace the supernal light that empowers this message, rarely will you be, if ever, traumatized by the effects of illness and disease.

Living from the expanse of the heart-mind will prevent you from resonating with the base vibrations associated with illness or disease, because dis-ease comes from being ill at ease with yourself. This is an important subject I wish to expand on in the following section, aptly named Developing Dis-eases.

Illness and disease continue to occur because our true spiritual (angelic) identity has and more importantly is, continually overshadowed by glamour-based illusion, materialism, expectation, and the worship of erroneous gods in doctrines and man-made religious dogma. Itnever ceases to amaze me when divine spirituality is mistakenly connected to modern-day religion. Unfortunately, the practices of many religions have lost sight of their original and intended purpose.

Our identity has also been eclipsed by an overall lack of heart-centered creativity. This is why there are very few original and uniquely creative ideas in the world today. Most ideas are muddied copies of something more significant. It is hoped that Neptune's current domicile transit of Pisces might reintegrate the divine essence—the long-lost creativity upon the Earth—which will re-harmonize the plane of the Earth. However, Neptune in Pisces may first need to cleanse the Earth from the sickly humanistic illnesses of greed, violence and corruption by purging it with the element of water. Greed, violence and corruption are the ultimate dis-eases.

The heart is continually marred with feelings of scepticism, uncertainty and doubt that are emanations of the head-mind. Most concerning is the fact that we have forgotten and lost sight of our spiritual heritage, and as a result have disassociated ourselves from the beautifully-coordinated divine consciousness—our true safe haven of spirituality. This loss was brought to culmination after centuries of discord by Neptune's recent transit of Aquarius—creating additional worldwide dis-ease. The actual purpose of this heavenly alignment was to realign our collective consciousness (Aquarius) with that of the divine (Neptune). This is why many souls on the plane of physicality are either unprepared, or in denial of the approaching Age of Aquarius.

In addition, illnesses and disease occur because we continue to negate our true physical and spiritual potential, which is cast in the horoscope or natal chart. The fact that so many people do not believe in astrology, or cite widespread ills with regards to its validity, or simply cannot comprehend it, is proof of just how much we remain contradictory to our spiritual roots and ultimate evolutionary potential. What an unfortunate state of affairs humankind finds itself in—arriving at the doorway of the spiritually-enhanced and opportunistic realm of the twenty-first century—eclipsed by the approaching and much-publicized Age of Aquarius.

Whether we chose to believe or disbelieve astrology, the planets each represent a wonderful expression of possibility that we, as the divine sparks of creation, created as spheres of potential millennia ago in our original angelic vibration. Our planet Earth upon which we all exist upon is a pivotal part of the energy bubble fenced in by the interconnected solar system, and that must be saved at all costs, even though it houses a multitude of illnesses and diseases that are altering its core evolutionary and spiritual purpose.

Similar to the beautifully exquisite beliefs held in the hearts of highly-evolved souls, and spiritually-minded astrologers such as Nancy B. Detweiler, and Alice Miller, I believe the natal chart signifies a cosmic blueprint for the soul's plan of action and a marker for evolutionary progression. Encompassed within its framework, is a set of circumstances that offers every human being valuable insight into the prevention of illness and disease. But the remedy of prevention will only become a viable option when we begin listening (via heart-centered meditation) to the soul's evolutionary message that resonates from the central plexus of the psyche: the mind of the heart.

If we are not tuned in to the correct frequency of the heart how can we possibly resonate with its universally-coordinated transmission? Essentially, illness and disease are the result of our refusal to listen to the supersensible dispatches of the heart-mind. Most of us prefer to tune in to the illusion that freely emanates from the mind.

The Indisposition of Dis-ease

Specific infirmities, which I refer to as: 'the developing dis-eases of the twenty-first century,' have been examined throughout this book along with many other associated conditions. Although these particular dis-eases have always been at the forefront of our existence, alarmingly they are now beginning to distend. These proliferating maladies became noticeable when humanity began the twenty-first century, the new millennium.

Representative of the multiple metabolic states, the dis-eases I am referring to primarily are dementia—fragmentation of the psychological bodies (representative of the cardinal signs: Aries, Cancer, Libra and Capricorn), depression—conducive to mental anguish and distress (representative of the mutable signs: Gemini, Virgo, Sagittarius and Pisces), and diabetes—malfunction of the physical surrounding body (representative of the fixed signs: Taurus, Leo, Scorpio and Aquarius).

Similar to the shortage of awareness surrounding other physical and mental indispositions, these particular dis-eases are the direct result of that lack of knowledge and common sense that seems to be evident throughout the world today, especially where diabetes is concerned. One individual I spoke to recently with regards to diabetes had never heard of the pancreas, not to mention its primary function in the body.

In addition, there is a comprehensive lack of awareness towards the necessity of healthy organic nutrition. Unfortunately, this lack of knowledge towards ethical nutrition seems to be an expanding issue, that is spreading like a virus throughout our modern but fragmented societies today. Civilizations that lack the harmony, balance and coherence required to sustain the need for the correct and sustainable nutrition are particularly affected, because they have become irresponsible in sustaining physical, mental, psychological and spiritual cohesion.

Disturbing Echoes of the New Millennium

Despite great anticipation, mankind reluctantly dipped his toe into the evolutionary waters of the twenty-first century, unaware of what to expect. Issues of immorality coupled with sublime levels of superficiality carried by previous generations for centuries have already left their vibrational resonance on the new millennium. Unfortunately, I fear the continuous expansion of these negative-based ills will further transform this multi-dimensional, technologically-advanced and liberating epoch into an age of disillusionment, destruction, apathy, perversion and expectation—similar to the inflicted trappings of the outgoing

Piscean Age. This fact will become personified if we make no attempt to reawaken and reclaim our long-forgotten spiritual heritage.³

Now that we have arrived at an important juncture in our collective evolution we should have eliminated the illusion associated with illness and disease. Yet, because of the apparent loss of our inherent spirituality we are creating dis-eases because of sullied thoughts and speculations, flawed belief systems, and negative assumptions—echoes from times long past—including the reintegration of illnesses and diseases that were previously contained.

Astrologers would no doubt agree that the reason many of us experience apathy, for example, on a grand scale, is because we find ourselves seated on the cusp of a major transformation—amely the changing of the Great Ages, from Pisces to Aquarius. A brief poetic description of the Age of Aquarius, aptly named "The New Kingdom," can be found at the front of this book.

Logically, this would explain why so many people have and are continuing to become robotic, losing the ability to think for themselves. However, this form of mental paralysis of losing one's mental faculties has always existed in one form or another throughout the ages. Recently, the echo of Neptune's transit of Aquarius continues to exacerbate the situation further, considering how many people now rely on their technological gadgets. Disturbingly, if this trend continues long into Pluto's ingress of Aquarius (ruling robots) beginning in 2024, it will point to a catastrophic worldwide influence where humans are systematically transformed into robots by their own free will.

Displaying robotic tendencies has become a disturbing trend amongst the younger generation of today, particularly the Neptune in Aquarius soul group referred to as: The Lost Generation. It is also becoming a problem amongst the elderly, particularly the Pluto in Cancer generation. This particular form of habitual robotics is referred to as dementia.

All of these factors are due to the misconceptions and the dismissal of Universal Law. If Universal Law was still a part of our soul reckoning there would be no illness and disease on the physical plane, and astrology would be regarded as a crucial tool for progression, as it was in ancient times.

Unrivalled Change

Meanwhile, as the energy streams signifying absolute change continue to vibrate on planet Earth many people will endeavour to lose their way in life. This is happening because a large percentage of souls have, on almost every conceivable level, forgotten their spiritual heritage. As a result, they no longer believe that their souls emanate from that elevated zone of consciousness many refer to as the divine—collective sparks of creation.

The first cycle of the new millennium that implicates Neptune's domicile transit of Pisces was intended to bring us back from the brink of self-destruction, disillusioned idealism, and ultimately back to God. Instead, and because of the field of energy surrounding the Earth set to negative, it is propelling many souls onto the tip of an enormous tidal wave of despair and ignominy. This is creating a confluence—a second tidal wave moving simultaneously, where greed, violence and corruption are awash over the Earth. This is what happens at a collective level when Neptune's vibration isn't elevated to the spiritual soul level.

Conversely, Neptune and Pisces' base vibrations representing disillusioned idealism, applies equally to individuals and groups that have become entrenched in the muddied perceptions of misguided and altered religions that are prevalent today. But similar to politics, the resonance vibrations of virtually every religion are beginning to dissipate and dissolve. This was a process that first began with Pluto's ingress of Sagittarius.

This transit caused a backwash that allowed these outdated teachings to reach a point of no return. This will become increasingly evident during the latter stages of Saturn's transit of Sagittarius (2015-2017) when a violent intent will be linked with some religions, causing a worldwide contagion of fear that will metastasize throughout outer related factors, and culminate during Saturn's conjunction with Pluto in Capricorn in 2020.

Meanwhile, a large percentage of souls at this time are not recognizing the purpose of the intensified rays of light that are being guided towards the Earth plane, transmitted by the elevated souls and co-workers of God. Spiritually this is another reason for Neptune's transit of Pisces, symbolizing that these beautifully-coordinated transitions are in fact occurring. Once again, these vibrations are not being utilized because the individual vibrations of many souls have not been raised sufficiently.

As a further consequence, this large percentage of souls are at serious risk of succumbing to the effects of illness and disease, especially from one of the designated dis-eases that will become noticeable in the early stages of the twenty-first century and will proliferate in the later stages of this evolutionary cycle of time. Ultimately, this extremely high percentage of people, the ones who are particularly at risk, can prevent these dis-eases from snowballing simply by raising their perception towards the divine conception of God and creation; and by raising their soul vibration of course.

Perhaps most concerning is that astrology has mostly been viewed as a misrepresentation of the truth and therefore dismissed in this way. Likewise, astrology is frequently disregarded as nonsense and not as an important part of a greater truth. Yet it is one of the few universal teachings symbolizing the truth, possessing the ability to purge and realign the soul, assisting it as it embraces spiritual enlightenment.

The enlightened souls who truly embrace the universal gift of astrology simply refuse to suffer the aftermath associated with the negative concept of disillusioned idealism, because these elevated souls are also in constant remembrance of Universal Law. Remembering Universal Law is pivotal to self-healing.

Karmic Law

If human beings exhibited their individual and collective thoughts from the mind of the heart there would be no illness or disease, and no karmic law, at least not in the traditional sense. Frequently, karma is discerned as *repetition*, if karma was viewed otherwise the negative constructs that surround illness and disease would cease to exist. There would be no poverty, apathy, greed or ignorance, and there would definitely be no discord in any fashion upon the plane of the Earth. Surely this would be a good enough reason to instil the construct of absolute change? One can always hope!

Unfortunately, because a greater percentage of individuals have forgotten their spiritual purpose, and the essence of who they are, they have somehow become misplaced in a bottomless pit of Neptunian illusion. A vast majority of humankind exists as a fragmented collective beset by misguided idealism and muddied humanistic beliefs, seemingly trapped on a dark cyclic tundra. Thus, humankind continues to survive on a ravaged and polluted planet living mostly in the confounds of excessive and impoverished societies, where the above issues continue to proliferate.

Is it ever likely that there will be less illness and disease on Earth? Evidently, the beliefs and traditions of mankind's flawed legacy are nothing new—they have been a constant force for millennia. But will we ever learn to ascend to a heightened level of consciousness? That is the question we must seriously ask ourselves before it is too late, and before Pluto (the end of days) completes its current cycle of the zodiac—around fifty years or so from this point.

It is my belief that many souls will endeavour to elevate their spiritual essence sufficiently before we arrive at the point where the Earth can no longer sustain us; the potential point of cataclysm. Pluto enters Aries in 2069. This is a potentially denunciatory juncture in our evolution signalling a time to reap what we have sown. The question is, has the evolutionary soil been suitably replenished, or has it been depleted of its life-sustaining nutrients?

Conditioned Beliefs

In order to understand the universal laws of divine spirituality, we must first eliminate the conditioned beliefs that have enveloped the human condition for millennia—the illusion and the corrupt trappings associated with perceived physicality. Illness and disease exist because of wrong thinking. Thoughts are truly powerful integers; human beings are capable of bringing illness into being simply through the power of thought. Illness and disease are often the direct result of negative and dissolute thinking.

In order to successfully unleash our forgotten spiritual heritage human beings must learn to love themselves completely from the mind of the heart, and start to believe in the miracle of creation instead of speculating about its questionable existence. Rightfully, this is what Neptune is attempting to show us as it journeys through its natural domain of Pisces.

The essence of a human being is composed of divine light comprising color coordinations. It is limitless and timeless. As bizarre as it sounds every human being on planet Earth is capable of embarking on a truly amazing journey into the heart of creation in order to discover their spiritual heritage, and astrology is a truly remarkable tool that has the potential to open the heart to the miracle of this latent possibility.

We are much more than finite physical beings subjected to systematic malfunction (dis-ease). Indeed, in our natural state we are truly remarkable beings that are both formless and infinite—if only we could remember. Neptune once again!

The Formless Concepts of Illusion (Misconceptions of Universal Law)

It is important to note that illness and disease do not occur by design; and they are not, contrary to the opinion of the medical profession in the form of human mishaps. We manifest them via our free will. In addition, speaking merely from a physical perspective, illness and disease are the result of vitamin and mineral deficiency in the natal chart (see Chapter 10, The Importance of Herbs, Vitamins and Minerals in the Natal Chart for more information).

Endnotes

[1] At its core, karmic law is an invitation so that experience can be gained. Today, in its skewed reality karmic law only applies to the human condition in its finite form. Universal Law is an entirely different concept and applies to the soul in its infinite reality. We are all angelic spiritual beings that have became encased in dense physical matter, the result of an experiment that went disastrously wrong millions of years ago aptly entitled the *fall*. Consequently, for the most part, we are trapped in a repeating cycle of incarnation bound by karmic law because that which is created on Earth must also be purged on Earth.

Until we begin remembering who we are and our spiritual heritage and thus break the cycle of physical incarnation, we will always be bound by karmic law. Illness and disease play significant role in this, as they are manifested by the disillusions of the head-mind. The heart-mind is the multiple energy structure that understands the emancipated creative choices that are the foundation premise of Universal Law.

[2] A reference to Alan Oken's excellent publication *Soul Centred Astrology*.

[3] For further information: www.josephspeaks.com

Chapter Three

Developing Dis-eases

"I am in the rhythm and flow of my ever-changing life, therefore I see my patterns, and I choose to make changes."—Louise L. Hay

Embracing the importance of the above affirmation would eliminate many, if not all, of the developing dis-eases that pervade the Earth plane. But alas, in this troubled and disconnected world, I cannot help feeling that the essence of this beautifully-affirmed discipline has dissolved through centuries of discord. When repeatedly spoken via meditation and prayer this affirmation is the epitome of self-healing.

Throughout this chapter, I have highlighted some of the most profound developing dis-eases that are directly associated with Neptune—one of the most difficult, mysterious and yet alluring planets of all. I have chosen to highlight Neptune's influence above all else because of its supple, invisible and powerfully-transcending influence, which is coming to the forefront now that it wields its supremacy from its domicile sign of Pisces.

Developing dis-eases are systematized imbalances. Developing dis-eases are also responsible for the noticeable surge in illness and disease.

Synopsis

The case studies that follow represent a cross-section of the psychological, mental and physical dis-eases that are widespread throughout the world today, along with the scars they leave behind that imprint an invisible residue on the landscape of the collective consciousness.

Metaphorically speaking, there is no difference between the physical dis-ease of extremism and the disease cancer. Some would say that extremism is a form of cancer. Both of these extremities cause maximum stress and imbalance, and in most cases they will terminate the life force—removing the free will of the individual in one form or another.

This Neptune-highlighted chapter merely outlines the causes of illness and disease categorizing them as "Developing Diseases." This is why I consider this chapter to be the foundation stone for the entire book. Meanwhile, the reason I have selected a particular cross-section of dis-eases throughout this publication is because of their growing commonality and alarming links to each other; and also because they have their roots buried deep in humankind's evolutionary past.

The evolutionary connections between these concerning diseases are examined in greater depth throughout Part Two , Prognosis.

Extremism

One of the oldest dis-eases that is again now developing is radical extremism. This is associated mostly with the planet Neptune and his mythical brother Pluto, because when these planets vibrate from their lowest capacity (see further on) they evoke the desire for power and control attained via obsessive tendencies. Extremism is the narrative of illusion-based martyrdom (Neptune). What is not widely reported is that the vibrations that emanate from extremism are having a ruinous effect upon the Earth, especially on its Neptune-ruled oceans.

The negative vibrations generated by extremism are directly responsible for the noticeable rise in weather anomalies such as hurricanes, underwater earthquakes and tidal waves (Neptune), and the severe loss of marine life as a result. It renders the Earth in a state of constant dis-ease, because the oceans are crucial to all life upon the Earth. The rise of extremism is also, in my opinion, responsible for the shifting jet streams, causing severe weather anomalies. Extremism opposes authority figures in the form of despots (Uranus); and Uranus rules the jet streams and earthquakes. This is another example of the Earth being in a constant state of dis-ease.

Meanwhile, the dark vibrational imbalance of the Earth plane caused by extremism and other developing dis-eases is accelerating illness and disease, collectively reaching alarming proportions throughout the world. Added to this, is the loss of marine life caused by the contamination of the oceans with plastic (Neptune), and other poisonous substances such as mercury, which enters the food chain generating more illness and disease.

Extremism is mostly associated with acts of violence frequently reported in the media, such as terrorism (Neptune). So what causes the initial imbalance in the brain that triggers the desire to commit violence? One example is the existence of poisonous substances in the brain. Consuming contaminated fish and drinking polluted water for example interferes with the production of endorphins that are released in the brain. Cutting off the supply of endorphins to the brain causes depression (see the end of this chapter), and depression is the foundation for other mental imbalances—triggers for violence.

Many of the acts of terrorism that the world has witnessed more recently have been orchestrated from Syria and Iraq—countries whose supplies have been polluted by noxious chemicals because of conflict and war.

Notably, extremism has increased threefold since Neptune (illusion and martyrdom) began tenanting its domicile sign of

Pisces. Developing dis-eases are being fabricated almost everywhere; primarily because of a lack of spiritual awareness underlined by Neptune in Pisces. We could deduce that this lack of spiritual awareness is in fact a developing dis-ease, but in essence it has been prevalent for millennia.

The on-going pollution of the world's oceans has become a developing dis-ease because the oceans are now in a state of consequential dis-ease. And so is humankind.

Overpopulation

Civilization has now reached a crisis point—caused mostly by overpopulation. The plight of overpopulation was emphasized by the Saturn/Neptune square of 2015 with the inclusion of the Jupiter T-square of 2017 that also encompassed Uranus and Pluto in the configuration. This T-square reactivated the recent squares that formed between Uranus and Pluto over a seven year period (seven being Neptune's number in numerology).

Countries are being overpopulated further by a rise in economic and illegal migration (Neptune). As a result of all this mass movement landmasses will erode causing the oceans to rise further. This alarming transition is now occurring along the coasts of the United Kingdom. Literally, the UK is dissolving, because of all the additional weight it has to support incurred by mass overpopulation. The UK is one example of a country that is severely and karmically dis-eased. Mythically speaking, and according to Neptune and Pisces operating at its lowest capacity (see further on), everything must eventually return to the sea to be purged.

Overall however, the presence of these powerful aspects are reminding mankind that urgent change, especially in the way we think, needs to be instilled if we are to prevent further damage to the natural environment. Overpopulation has never existed in the extremes it has reached today; therefore the concept of overpopulation is and continues to be a developing dis-ease. Overpopulation will proliferate unless a solution is found to prevent any further imbalance occurring on the Earth plane.

Overpopulation is a precursor for illness and disease, because overpopulation generates a lack of basic necessities, such as food and shelter. A psychological fear of being without is set in stone in the subconscious. Because of global overpopulation, food shortages and homelessness in the rich countries of the west are set to become developing dis-eases if things do not change drastically.

The one advantage connected to overpopulation is healing. Collectively, seven billion Aquarian souls can heal the planet faster than two billion dysfunctional ones. This can only occur if we raise our individual and collective awareness towards the conviction of change, as eloquently expressed by Louise Hay. In that case inwardly seeking Neptune in its domicile sign of Pisces is there purely to assist with this spiritual transition.

Arduous Aspects: Absolving the Ego

I now wish to highlight the purpose of arduous aspects; sometimes referred to as frictional aspects, because as a worst case scenario arduous aspects (operating at the lowest capacity) are responsible for the emergence of developing dis-eases.

The most widely acknowledged astrological aspects in this group are: the opposition, the quindecile, the quincunx, the sesquiquadrate, the square, the semi/square and the semi/sextile aspects. Despite the opinion of many, I do believe that on occasion the semi-sextile can pose as a difficult aspect, especially when we are unaware of its influence or when we simply refuse to work with it constructively. For now though I begin my analysis with the quincunx aspect and the ramifications—chiefly because of its underestimated and unrecognized values. When operating at its lowest capacity the quincunx is perhaps the aspect above all that prevents self-healing.

The quincunx has always struck a cosmic chord with me and

holds for me a source of extreme fascination. Quincunxes are a major factor in the onrush of the developing dis-ease scenario.

Operating at the Lowest Capacity

When we choose to live life at a pace that holds a distinct lack of conscious awareness, for example when we chose to live life in the fast lane, the arduous aspects will only vibrate from their lowest vibrational capacity. This being the case, we should expect to be affected significantly by these low energy base vibrations, especially when we find ourselves under the influence of the quincunx and the square (both exceptionally testing aspects when operating at their lowest capacity). For many, living life in the fast lane is an accepted way of life; however it is nonetheless categorized as a developing dis-ease.

When influenced significantly by the raw vibrations of the arduous aspects, the negative effects upon the physical body can be acute—raising the prospect of illness and disease. Illness and disease occurs because these base negative vibrations minimize the protection of the body's immune system. In addition, arduous aspects operating at their lowest base capacity, have a malign effect on the Earth because the immune system of the planet has been severely depleted. One example of this is the continually shifting jet streams. The shifting jet streams have now become a developing dis-ease.

At worse arduous aspects expend the body's fundamental defences, particularly the quincunx, the sesquiquadrate and the square. The sesquiquadrate is a very difficult aspect to master; my analogy for this aspect is that it represents the straw that broke the camel's back.

The prospect of illness and disease increases when the quincunx is observed in the natal chart. Quincunxes are frequent in death charts, as are oppositions, whose effects mimic the quincunx by having planets that tenant disassociating signs. Paradoxically, quincunxes and squares are widely acknowledged as healing aspects, so I have categorized them in the following order further in Chapter 7.

The quincunx and its twinned aspect, the semi-sextile, are in effect inconjuncts (see footnote 1, Chapter 1, for a brief explanation about inconjuncts). These often undervalued aspects operate in a very supple capacity and should never be dismissed as irrelevant. The power they emit can often be demeaning, addictive and certainly life-altering, as we shall observe for the quincunx in the following case examples.

The Cumulative Effects of the Quincunx

The quincunx or 150-degree asymmetric aspect receives little or no recognition, yet it represents a key influence for self-*healing* and evolutionary progress. When this planetary disposition is identified in the natal chart a necessary *adjustment* is required in a specific area upon the life path. In essence, the individual seeks to adopt an entirely nascent perspective so that the soul can encompass a wholly new set of circumstances to aid healing and progression.

Perhaps the quincunx signifies a type of cosmic compass pointing to facets of the persona that remain karmically unpolished. Alternatively, quincunxes highlight gray zones indicating confusion, hence impasses of energy—conceivably something that hindered the soul's evolutionary progression, now requiring atonement. Either way the quincunx is vitally important because its purpose it to *rebalance* the karma the soul has agreed to undertake.

Keywords

- Difficult attributes—lack of perspective and boredom, strain, obfuscating, challenging, antagonistic, abrasion, antipathy, asperity.
- Constructive attributes—redirecting, reorganising, adjustment, symmetry, transformation, conversion, reconstruction, releasing and balancing karma.

The Quincunx: A Cosmic Enigma

Overall, the planets or points involved in the quincunx do not understand each other. Thus, quincunxes are routinely observed as planetary alignments possessing adverse and frictional qualities—traditionally viewed as aspects of "disproportionate irregularity" that require the honing of deeper awareness. This is in some respect why I chose to project this aspect in greater detail. In medical astrology, quincunxes are pivotal influences as they are directly concerned with the onset of illness and disease. However, the vibrational resonance emitted by the quincunx is not clear; and for the most part its definition remains incomprehensible. It is often difficult to know what direction to take when under the influence of this aspect.

For the most part quincunxes are considered to be minor aspects—possessing energies that are seemingly inferior. However, in my opinion, the energy released by this critical aspect is "impacting." Quincunxes invariably point to the principal affliction or adjustment, implying a shift on the life path to avoid fatal errors in judgement, and to highlight potential intrusion of illness. If illness, disease or tragedy becomes an issue, the energy of the quincunx may become an overwhelming force. This is frequently observed in decumbiture, disaster and death charts—each chronicling the natal chart.

Expiration

If quincunxes feature in death charts the type of adjustment needed is one that requires an accepted transition from the physical Earth plane to the spirit world that, ideally, would be applied at the spiritual level because the death chart is merely a projection of the soul's passing.

Similarly, if quincunxes feature in a decumbiture chart the required adjustment is a change that is often needed on the life path in order that the physical body can be restored to good health. When quincunxes feature in the natal chart they signify

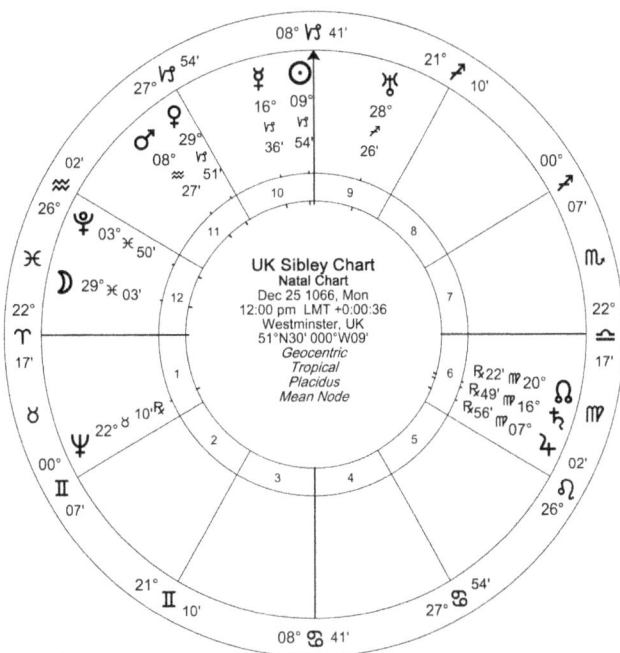

clauses in the karmic contract—a stringent reiteration of change is required—primarily because the soul experienced periods of stagnation in a past life. It may be that an individual had become *addicted* to alcohol and other stimulants in past lives; and therefore the cycle is repeating itself.

Metaphorically speaking, quincunxes are evolutionary reminders outlining the presence of unpaid taxes that are now due for payment to the creator so to speak. This would imply that the soul needs to be reawakened—reminding it of its spiritual roots, because the chord that attaches it to the Earth plane needs to be severed. Quincunxes imply that the soul's true home lies in the spirit world; and it is the spirit world that becomes the source of confusion for many today.

Likewise, when quincunxes are observed in natal charts a *major adjustment* in the course of a lifetime is required, especially in the areas determined by the planets, houses and adjoining aspects. Quincunxes are particularly potent if the houses that accommodate the planets are intercepted, or in angular houses. Quincunxes culminate at an exactitude of 150 degrees in disassociate signs; with an orb of 2/3 degrees. Perhaps, this is a further reason why this aspect can have a detrimental effect on the health of an individual, though essentially the quincunx represents an aspect of healing, as do all planetary aspects that are considered to be exacting. But before healing can take effect the challenges set by the quincunx must be triumphed over. Ultimately, quincunxes are symptomatic of the all-embracing pre-set challenge—coupled by a nebulous intonation.

Neptunian Influences

The quincunx is, in my humble opinion, a Neptune aspect, because quincunxes cause misdiagnosis and addiction.

In June 2017 the World Health Organization (WHO, see natal chart) reported a sharp increase in alcohol-related illnesses since the start of the year.[1] The report also highlighted a rise in liver cancer and kidney disease. At the time of this announcement an unusually-lengthy quincunx between Jupiter in Libra and Neptune in Pisces had reached its exactitude for the third and final time, after it initially formed in April 2017. Hence that popular saying in astrology: "third time pays for it all." Both these planets are the rulers of Pisces—making the influence of the quincunx extremely significant.

A large part of the nature of this quincunx was to highlight the extreme levels of alcohol and drug consumption blighting the world today, and all in the name of apathy—falsely appearing as glamorized socializing (Jupiter and Neptune). Jupiter rules the liver, and Libra rules the kidneys, and Neptune in Pisces epitomizes the illusion associated with chemical addictions, that in realty cause damage to the liver and kidneys and lower limbs via the lymphatic system. Alcohol and drug-related problems are

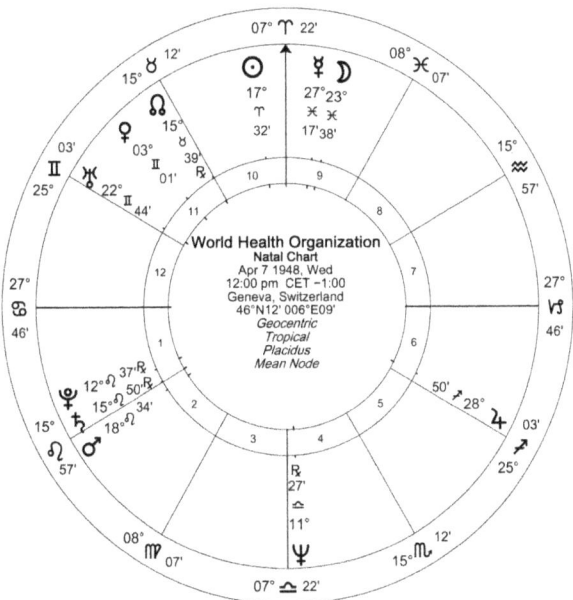

becoming a global epidemic and this is why I thought it prudent to highlight the causes and dangers throughout this particular section. Somehow these disillusioned concepts need to be adjusted (a quincunx keyword) via renewed spiritual awareness combined with hope (Pisces and Neptune).

Saturn's 2017 transit of Sagittarius is attempting to deliver an important message, where increased responsibility and awareness is needed more than ever if we are to progress as a collective, especially at this time of sublime chemical abuse and enhanced disillusion (Neptune). It seems that today many people simply bury their heads in the sand of alcohol and drug abuse, especially when they are confronted with stress-related adversity.

Accepting responsibility for one's actions in a world that is rife with injustice, outrage and sin, is what Saturn is attempting to convey during its tenure of happy-go-lucky Sagittarius. With Saturn in Sagittarius it's about splitting the arrow, using the concepts of pressure and time. The "split arrow" syndrome ultimately destroys the conviction of irresponsibility; and irresponsibility has long been designated as a developing dis-ease.

Once the arrow has been repaired using the strong-bonding solvent of Saturn it will be able to travel much further because it will be stronger by design; and its archer will be more responsible and acute with his aim. The Saturn/Sagittarian cycle will reach its point of culmination during Saturn's domicile transit of Capricorn in 2018-2020, at which point we will all see the effects of its Sagittarius transit.

The unusual duration of the quincunx was due, in part, to both planets altering direction, with Neptune turning retrograde and Jupiter turning direct at approximately the same time. However, this cosmic phenomenon would have further repercussions across the global spectrum mainly because of the levels of nonprogression (a developing dis-ease) mankind freely wallows in. Here is one example of its negative effects:

Drug Abuse: The Ultimate Developing Dis-ease

At the 2017 Glastonbury music festival (music being ruled by Neptune), in the southwest of England, it was reported that at least three deaths had occurred through overdosing on "hippy crack" (the latest craze amongst New Age revellers). Hippy crack (a Neptune substance) is now designated as a class B drug, and is purchased often illegally in separate canisters and mixed with nitrous oxide (laughing gas). The combined elements are then inhaled from balloons in order to provide the optimum euphoric effect. This euphoria effect is often self-perpetuating, as opposed to self-healing. In its worse case scenario hippy crack has an overwhelming effect on the brain causing epileptic type convulsions (see Chapter 4) and paralysis.

In addition, hippy crack, especially when mixed with nitrous oxide, is lethal when compounded with extensive alcohol consumption. At the time of these unfortunate events Mars in Cancer had made an exact square to Jupiter and was applying its influence to Neptune via a trine. Interestingly, the attendees of this year's Glastonbury festival remarked that "this is where we feel most at home" (Cancer).

Operating from its lower base vibration these tragic events were underlined by the quincunx influenced by illusionary Neptune. Since Neptune's transit of Pisces began in 2011 the use of illegal and the misuse of prescription drugs has almost quadrupled (Saturn). These alarming statistics echo the binge drinking culture that formed at the beginning of Neptune's transit of Pisces.

Speaking from an evolutionary perspective, this configuration was attempting to convey a need for "adjustment" in the way we search for and recognize our connection with God (Jupiter and Neptune). The quincunx represented an alternative route to the way we attain happiness and direction (Jupiter), namely looking into the spiritual heart for guidance and getting free from the shackles of alcohol and drug addiction (Neptune).

In the United Kingdom's preferred 12:00 noon 1066, Westminster chart (see chart below) the 2017 quincunx aspect highlights a growing wave of anti-social behaviour and obesity (Jupiter), fuelled by alcohol and drug addiction, which was karmic in nature (Saturn and Neptune). This would seem to indicate that the United Kingdom has contracted a contagion-type illness of unprecedented magnitude, afflicted by the deadly virus of sin (a developing dis-ease amongst society). This contagion would in turn begin to cripple its healthcare resources, such as the National Health Service (NHS and Neptune).

Often when the need for an adjustment is not foreseen the consequences can be catastrophic. It makes the adjustment-orientated quincunx a very potent and important aspect; and is, in my opinion, a major aspect.

Temptation and Rehabilitation

Quincunxes operating at their lowest base level represent the fuel needed to ignite temptation. It is my opinion that the overall effects of the quincunx reflect the planet Neptune because temptation is a Neptune facet. Temptation is the catalyst for alcohol and drug addiction, making it the unfortunate instrument for mental illness and liver and kidney disease.

Alternatively, when we chose to listen to the calling of the heart, via the application of free will, we instinctively raise the soul's vibration to a much higher and more responsive frequency, causing the soul to shine aurally. As a result, divine light is projected through the aural energy field encompassing the physical body allowing the process of healing to begin on all levels of consciousness. This marks the sacred distinction of soul rehabilitation—another Neptune facet.

Some will confess categorically that the body enters into this natural euphoric state when under the influence of heavy drug or alcohol consumption. This is perhaps the real reason why so many people regularly consume alcohol and drugs in order to experience this exultant state of being. Unfortunately, this is merely an illusion created by artificial substances (Neptune), and therefore has nothing to do with the heart.

Euphoria attained by artificial stimulants can be designated as a developing dis-ease, equally caused by the effects of Neptune operating from its lowest base vibration. This profoundly marks the fallacious undertaking of soul temptation—yet another Neptune facet.

As previously remarked upon the quincunx is an aspect with an orb of 150 degrees, and when these numbers are multiplied they add up to 6. Six is Venus's number in numerology (see Chapter 6); and Venus has been designated as Neptune's lower octave vibration in esoteric astrology. Also, from Venus ruled-Libra to Neptune ruled-Pisces in the zodiac is 150 degrees—marking a natural quincunx aspect. With that in mind perhaps a further notion that could be highlighted here is that Venus represents temptation of the physical body, and therefore the fallout from that temptation reverberates through the spiritual body of Neptune creating major implications.

Gout for example, is a disease that affects the feet and the toes (Neptune and Pisces) and its cause is traditionally associated with heavy alcohol consumption, particularly red wine and ruby port. The feet are an essential part of the spiritual body because they reflect the body's organs via the meridian points; therefore they are directly connected to the soul chakras. In the long-term gout has a detrimental effect on the kidneys (Venus and Libra).

According to the World Health Organisation (WHO see chart below) gout has increased throughout the western world in the last 20 years, therefore designating it as most certainly a developing dis-ease. In the foundation chart of the World Health Organisation we see a strongly emphasized sixth house of health. Domicile Jupiter resides there. From the sixth house, Jupiter and Sagittarius need to relay awareness and direction, and to deliver (via its arrows) information all over the world. With the Cancer Ascendant there is a need to nurture the world's health from her bosom.

Visualizing the natural colors associated with the quincunx, particularly white and ivory, around the affected area will help to neutralize the effects of gout (for more information about colors refer to Chapter 12).

Let us briefly examine the natal chart of Susan Boyle whose life has been heavily influenced by the quincunx; and who also suffers from gout.

Susan Boyle

Quincunxes are often a prelude to developing dis-eases in the natal chart. To better understand the challenging potential of the quincunx let us now explore the chart of the spirited but almost-forgotten singer Susan Boyle, whose life has been shadowed and dominated by this cosmic enigma. The quincunx is the basis for developing dis-eases in the form of mental health problems.

Most strikingly, perhaps, is that her natal chart reveals the Sun in Aries (exalted) at 11 degrees from the eleventh house where it forms a powerful quincunx to Neptune at 10 Scorpio in the

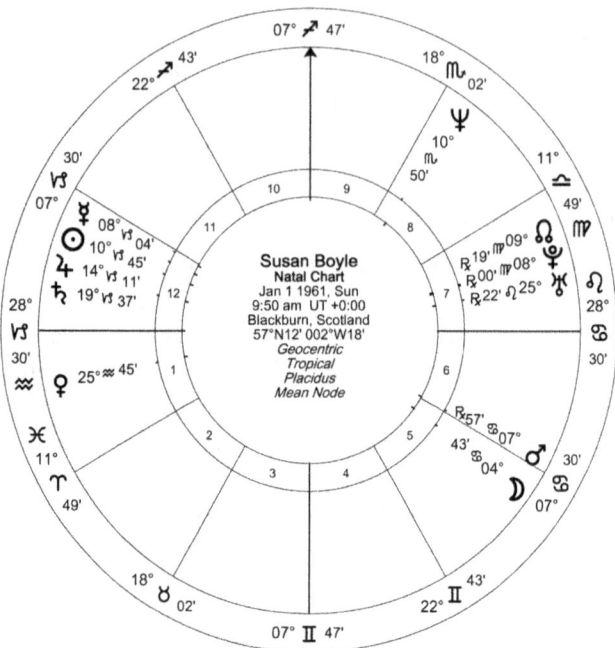

sixth house (using Placidus houses see natal chart 1). This particular quincunx is the quintessential component of the entire chart. Also connected is the Moon in Libra opposing the Aries Sun indicating the need for peace and harmony over conflict in her life. The inner turmoil caused by this configuration must be relinquished if she is to triumph over her on-going mental health problems brought on by the loss of a parent when she was ten years old (Sun/Moon opposition).[2]

Susan Boyle won the reality TV show *Britain's Got Talent* on April 11, 2009. The triggers were the transiting North Node in Aquarius (ruled by Uranus), and Pluto's transit of Capricorn. Between them these began influencing the natal quincunx via square aspects, hence the North Node to natal Neptune orchestrating irrationally fanciful hopes and wishes, and Pluto to her natal Sun causing great change (see chart for win). Transiting Jupiter had hitherto formed a square to Neptune.

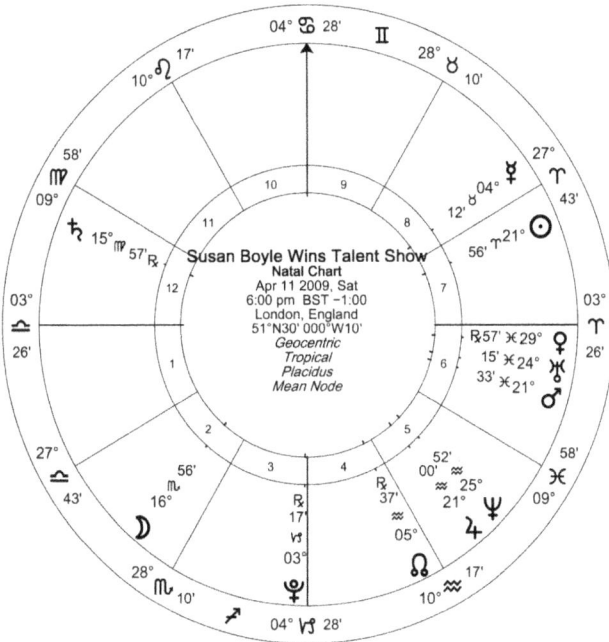

Her suddenly acquired fame and new direction (transiting Node to her natal Neptune), meant that she would need to transform her stature (transiting Pluto to her Sun) and adjust her lifestyle to this new glamorous image (Neptune) in order to accommodate her role now as a professional singer. This would prove difficult. Susan was soon branded a recluse by the media (Neptune in Scorpio) and the prospect of change proved a tall order to implement. Unfortunately, Susan's new-found singing career would be cut short by ongoing mental health issues, including Asperger's syndrome, and she found it difficult to make the adjustment the media required of her (transiting Aquarius North Node).

As mentioned previously the Sun and Moon are in opposition on her chart with the Moon tenanting the balanced sign of Libra. Overall this determines a person with a delicate and sensitive persona. Susan has suffered from anxiety disorder for

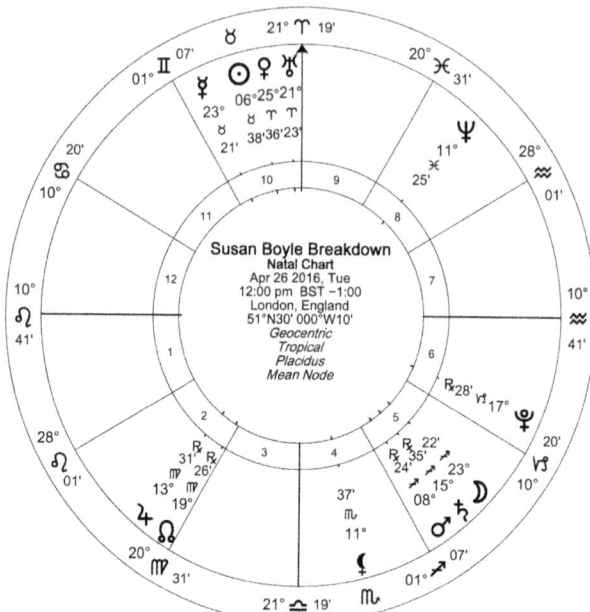

the most part of her life, a direct result of this opposition, plus the Sun/Neptune quincunx and the inclusion of a natal Saturn quincunx to her Ascendant. In addition, detrimental Mars, in its fall in Cancer signifying low levels of energy, sits at the apex of a natal T-square involving the Sun and Moon that joins with the Sun-Neptune quincunx. This powerful configuration is likely to have played a hand in her ongoing mental health problems and low self-esteem.

Some time ago, Susan suffered a complete mental and physical breakdown due to stress, caused in part by a transiting Jupiter opposition to Neptune (see chart for breakdown). Also, we see from this chart the Moon conjoined with the Part of Fortune[3] in quincunx to Mercury (travel) in an exact formation in Jupiter's sign of Sagittarius. The stellium of Sagittarius opposes the Ascendant in the natal chart. It is this combination of adverse aspects that, in my opinion, caused this breakdown—fuelled by guilt and her failed attempt to become a celebrity perhaps.

Additional Chart Delineation

- Natal Chart: Adjustment to Service. Saturn is another key player here because it influences her Ascendant via a quincunx from its dignified sign of Capricorn from the intensified fortress of the eighth house of transformation in Placidus. This quincunx is perhaps the catalyst for her gout Also, Saturn connects to the Sun via a quintile aspect, meaning she must ideally seek out a higher purpose to her life evoking a new set of ideals, healing and transmutation. Resisting the call of the evolutionary adjustment posed by the natal quincunxes may have increased the onset of mental illness, exacerbated by the Gemini Ascendant nearing 29 degrees, denoting a critical degree.

- Wins Talent Show: Denoting Self-Sacrifice. Similar to a lightning bolt from the heavens Susan unexpectedly wins a talent show—emphasized by the transiting North Node in Aquarius square to natal Neptune. Also, the natal Sun at the head of the quincunx tenants the eleventh house, opposite fifth house of entertainment at the midpoint of Neptune and Pluto. This chart suggested that a sudden temporary adjustment was required, but was the sudden Uranian influence too much for her fragile mind to acknowledge?

- Breakdown at Heathrow: Purporting the Outcome. In this event chart Jupiter connects to the natal Sun via a wide quincunx. Interestingly, in the months leading up to her winning the talent show Jupiter had squared the natal quincunx via Neptune. Perhaps this had a wider influence on her breakdown, especially as it occurred at an airport with Jupiter having rulership over aircraft. Also, the transiting Sun and Ascendant squares natal Neptune. Perhaps, all of this is the aftermath of an incorrect adjustment that she chose to pursue, and one that is solely based on illusion (Neptune).

Conclusion

Realistically, the fundamental and transformational adjustment required by the natal quincunx demands that in order to recognize her creative abilities (Moon in the fifth); she must ignite the flame of her heart as her spiritual guide in order to see her way through the fog of Neptune, and embrace the humanitarian potential of her natal sixth house coupled with her natal eleventh house Sun. It is reasonable to suggest however that Susan is capable of working with disadvantaged children.

In any case, Susan has exceptional abilities honed from past lives. This is determined by the two bi-quintiles and the quintile in kite formation with Pluto and the North Node at the Apex in Virgo with Chiron opposing in Pisces in the natal chart—exemplifying the Neptune wound—that can be healed through divine service to humanity. Pluto also rules her sixth house, hence a mark of a true and evolutionary humanitarian.

Winning the talent show was in many ways *unfortunate*, it was later reported that she had auditioned as a bet.[4] Yet it was also a stepping stone to prepare her for the humanitarian work she *should* ideally have undertook. This karmic test was set in motion at birth by natal Saturn in the transformational eighth house. In essence, Susan Boyle is not suited to a life in show business because it augmented her mental illness including her Asperger's syndrome—something that she may never fully recover from despite the heavenly grand trine that blesses her natal chart.

Discovering her true vocation through the redirecting influence of her quincunxes would surely have offered a cure, and one that allowed her the benefit of overcoming the debilitating mental illnesses that has, so far, plagued her life. And finally, to coin Susan's winning song on *Britain's Got Talent* I Dream the Dream, if this had been the case, then appropriately the dream certainly would not have turned into a nightmare for her.

Unfortunately, it was reported recently that Susan Boyle has retired from singing despite the release of her new album: Wonderful World. This is due to the worsening effects of her Asperger's syndrome.[5] Thus, for Susan Boyle the nightmare appears to be ongoing. In essence her Asperger's syndrome has become a developing dis-ease.

Causality

What is clear however is that for such a supposedly minor influence the impact conveyed by the quincunx should never be underestimated, or indeed repudiated.

The Importance of Astrology

As previously indicated in the Author's Note, astrology is an excellent tool that complements and assists the process of self-healing—raising the soul's vibration. Once we raise our levels of consciousness we can no longer be affected by the base vibrations generated by the hard aspects (opposition, quincunx, square etc). Instead, we can expect them to assist towards the process of soul advancement—catalysts for light energy.

Contrary to popular opinion, the onset of illness and disease can be a wondrous and purposeful transition. This is because all aspects of physical and mental afflictions and manifestations are specifically created by the soul for the purpose of awakening and spirit transcension.

In some cases, illness and disease are coerced into existence because the journey in life has taken some unnecessary diversions, where the soul has lost its way as a result of distractions or temptations. On occasion this loss of direction is designed to be a mechanism to guide the soul back to its true purpose of healing. Therefore, in some cases, it is a necessary process.

I used the word "distractions" because for the most part the diversions set up on this freewheeling no-limits highway of life that is now the Earth plane, are not an integral part of the karmic plan that is agreed before incarnation. Unplanned distractions (such as drug and alcohol abuse and the craving of the flesh for the purpose of perversion) are the result of sheer temptation; and temptation should be avoided. Temptation needs to be avoided particularly when Neptune and Venus are aspected to the Sun, Moon, Venus or the Ascendant via a square, quincunx or opposition in the natal chart.

The avoidance of temptation can be successfully achieved through the positive application of Saturn responsibility—achieved through his little acknowledged rewards of time and maturity. Neptune energy should only be applied successfully when the soul's vibration is raised sufficiently via the mastering (Neptune) of frictional aspects. Neptune self-healing is achieved by transcending apathy into bliss. Chemical addiction is the result of apathy, and bliss is a projection of contentment. Neptune opens the spiritual eye so that the individual can see forever. A fitting testament to the remembrance of the divine!

And finally Saturn reaffirms that having to endure the discomforts associated with illness and disease should ideally bring us to a point of realisation that impels us to rediscover our unique evolutionary path. This is a part of the karmic path that was purposely assigned via the application of our own free will to every soul in incarnation.

The Flawed Ego

The ego is a pestilential bi-product (Neptune) of the body's DNA sequences (Pluto). The ego can be likened to a shadowy imprint of our incoherent and ingrained time-held beliefs and conditionings—those facets of our persona that we refuse to relinquish because they represent power (Pluto).

Arduous aspects such as the square, sesquiquadrate, quincunx and the opposition (the ego aspects) should ideally be transcended into a vibration that is harmonious and thoughtful (Venus Pluto's polarity), and one of opportunistic potential in the natal chart, rather than merely suppressing these aspects as grand representations of the ego.

The ego is most definitely the blind spot, the Achilles heel (Neptune). Fatal flaws and weaknesses in the ego, such as mental health tendencies, are also indicated by the frictional planetary alignments in the natal chart. These aspects, operating at their lowest base resonant vibration, represent karmic imprints or impressionable indentations, which frequently manifest as serious mental health problems.

Mental health problems only exist because the ego has been dented or bruised in some way. Mental health problems are carried in the DNA profile and are brought back into manifestation from past incarnations (Saturn, Neptune and Pluto). So, with some required work, the arduous aspects do help to purge the ego. Alternatively, if we fail or refuse to purge the ego, we place ourselves (via free will) in a precarious and damming position once we return to the spirit world. The ego remains "flawed."

One astrological example of the flawed ego concept would be the Sun aligning with Mars via a square or opposition. As the worst case scenario, the Sun would receive no adjoining trines, quintiles, sextiles or even deciles at the same time to act as buffer zones.

This configuration may suggest that the ego is bruised (probably from a past life incarnation), and Mars would represent an unstoppable force of potentially self-destructive and violent energy—an appropriate catalyst for guilt and an incurring mental health condition.

Oscar Pistorius

This surge in negative energy has been highlighted recently with the highly-publicised trial and impending imprisonment of the South African Paralympic athlete Oscar Pistorius for the murder of his girlfriend Reeva Steemkamp in 2013 (for more information refer to my articles published in ISAR in 2016 and the New Zealand Federation of Astrology in 2017). In his natal chart Oscar Pistorius has an anaretic Sun[6] at 29 degrees joined to

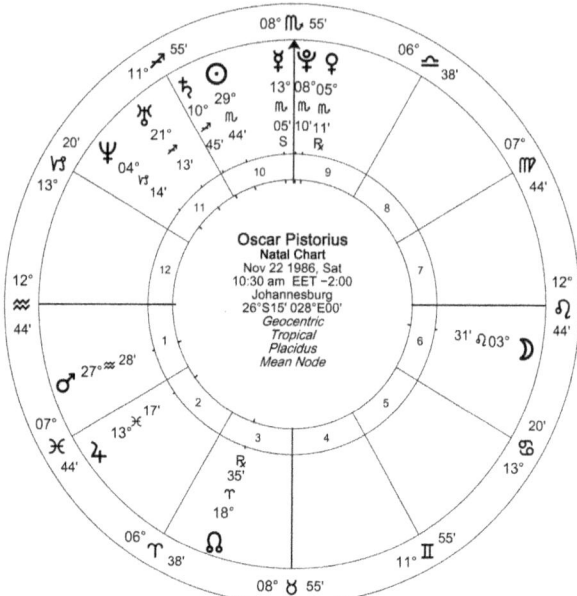

a domiciled Mars by a square (Mars in his first house) that was also affected by the transiting Sun on the morning of the murder (see natal chart below).

Of course there were contributing factors linking this square to other aspects of his chart. But this one single aspect would indicate the presence of the flawed ego. In retrospect, Oscar Pistorius is mentally ill. His natal chart bears all the hallmarks of borderline schizophrenia and borderline personality disorder (see Chapter 4 for more information about these diseases). The flawed ego also reflects narcissistic personality disorder, which is on the increase; therefore I would designate this 'flawed ego' syndrome as a developing dis-ease.

Healing

Neptune rules hospitals and hospitals are traditionally associated with healing. However, hospital admissions often occur under duress, which is likely to be the result of the flawed ego gripped by fear; and fear is invariably linked with Saturn. Pluto's influence, especially during a transiting sextile to a personal planet, can help the physical body circumvent illness or disease and alongside his brother Neptune it can provide the necessary healing.

Once the flawed ego is purged of all negativity and liberated from the entrenchment and attachment of illusion (Neptune at its lowest vibration), the belief in illness and disease is finally relinquished. To purge the flawed ego, visualize blue or violet light, centring it on the crown chakras.

Time Transits

An additional factor of demanding aspects is that they are simply meant to slow us down for the purpose of contemplation (Neptune and Pluto). Demanding aspects decrease the flow of wind that passes through our evolutionary sails, to put it metaphorically, especially when the aspect has the combined influences of implying Saturn, and the mastery of Neptune and transformational Pluto.

When illness and disease are a result of one or more arduous Saturn, Neptune and Pluto transits, the whole process can be an essential healing transition. In which case, Saturn the planet of confinement will place us in a Neptune-ruled hospital for a specific duration of time (Saturn) for the purpose of contemplation and transformation (Pluto).

Equally, Saturn has the capability of placing us in a Neptune-ruled spiritual healing center. This is especially relevant when a quincunx or semi-sextile connects these diversely opposite planets. A transition of this type occurs so that a time-based adjustment can be adhered to and transcended in the appropriate way. Maybe an impeding illness has brought about new levels of awareness in the individual whereby there is a perceived desire (Neptune) to perform some kind of secular humanitarian work. Of course this is perceived purely via the level of Saturn maturity and evolutionary progression (Pluto) attained by the individual concerned.

Time in Motion

Whereas time appears to slow down under the heavy influence of a Saturn transit, it appears to transgress in the opposite direction when propelled under the influence of a Uranus transit; particularly when these planets are aspected via a square, quincunx and opposition.

The acceleration and deceleration of time theory is an optical illusion. *Tempus fugit*, meaning "time flies like the wind," would be indicative of an unyielding Uranus transit, especially when the planet transits the luminaries or domiciled Mercury. Unfortunately, the negative displacement of Uranus means that its presence can impede the body's natural healing process, preferring to send the body into meltdown—notably via shock, seizure and spasm.

Likewise, Neptune transits can also impede the body's healing process, especially when this planet has not been elevated sufficiently to the soul level of consciousness (more about this further on). Neptune has no authority over conventional time—only the moment called now! Illness and disease can also occur because the individual believes there is simply not enough time to achieve personal goals. This familiar concept must now be designated as a developing dis-ease. Aside from Neptune, every planet in the natal chart requires their energies to be elevated to the soul level in order that karmic healing (in the absence of time) can be initialized.

The process of ascension requires a lifetime of Earth time if it is to be successfully achieved—overseen by Neptune. When soul ascension is refuted it is often replaced with the onset of illness and disease, which in my opinion, is orchestrated by Neptune. In addition, when elevated to a higher level of consciousness Neptune's purpose is to heal the soul by dissolving the external and the troublesome flawed ego.

The Time Field

The time field is an energy shield that encompasses the Earth. It is ruled by Saturn partly because Saturn is the skin that protects and holds everything in its rightful place. The time field is presently set to negative; the after-effects of millions of years of discord. The time field was installed to protect and energize our wellness when the Earth was viewed spiritually as a physical paradise. Since the altering of the field to negative, illness and disease have become prevalent factors upon the Earth. This is because the Earth plane is a very dis-eased place.

As a result of this unfortunate occurrence, demanding aspects will have an adverse effect upon our status, our direction, and more importantly perhaps, upon our wellbeing. The intense negative vibrations emitted by challenging aspects often cancel out the positive qualities that are rudimentary as a result of the time field.

Relying too much on conventional time in order to conduct our lives, which is what arduous aspects, particularly those governed by Saturn and Neptune at their base level imply, has now surely become a developing dis-ease across the fragmented global expanse of the Earth plane.

Expressive Aspects

Now that I have examined the challenging effects generally associated with the arduous aspects I will deliberate further on a group of aspects termed "expressive." I will begin my analysis with the most well-known of them all, the all-endearing trine.

Trines: Projections of Creativity

The trine is perhaps the most revered of all the expressive aspects because it forms the backdrop to the harmonious patterns of the cosmos. Trines are very Neptunian aspects! However, the trine's actual purpose can be misconstrued (more on this further on) but effectively it represents a source of euphonious energy with the potential to transcend the flawed ego from the plane of negative self-doubt to the plane of positive self-mastery—complete with renewed creativity.

Trines symbolize soulful vibrations of astute and inventive energy. Trines are healing aspects, particularly effective when they connect to arduous aspects in the natal chart. Similar to the sextile (see Chapter 7), trines need to be activated, otherwise their true potential can be easily overlooked or even repudiated. This is perhaps the main reason why trines are frequently misunderstood. Expressive aspects need to be activated because their ease of character means they can be easily dismissed or taken for granted, unlike the arduous aspects that often terrify us like an approaching tornado.

When a trine remains inactive its energy remains indolent. As a result trines symbolize voids in the natal chart that represent a manifestation of inert energy. Thus it becomes an aspect without any specific guidance or purpose; a source of inertia. All too often the opportunities posed by the trine are inadvertently viewed as something that requires little or no effort, and this view can seriously undermine its progressive potential. In that case, trines can pose more of a problem in the natal chart than the arduous aspects, simply because of the ease factor that they manifest. Being aware of embracing its soulful potential (via stillness) is perhaps the easiest way to activate the all-endearing trine.

From an esoteric viewpoint, trines indicate talents that have been successfully honed in past lives. If there are Grand Trines in the natal chart, the past life accumulated talents are multiplied threefold. The presence of a Grand Trine can imply great dexterity, yet within its central matrix (soul energy) can be the negative component of effortlessness.

Unfortunately, this sinful constituent of laziness has become a prevalent issue across the world today; therefore I designate it as a developing dis-ease.

The Karmic Plan

When the challenges posed by the frictional aspects are overcome and finally conquered (particularly the squares and oppositions under the influence of Neptune and Pluto), those facets of the soul requiring karmic transformation in this life should, ideally, be acuminated. The effects of the overcome square for example will be displayed in a natal chart in a future incarnation as the trine, providing of course that the soul has a distinct inclination to return to the Earth plane.

Unfortunately, if the potential bearing trine has not been successfully utilized in the natal chart and the opportunities missed or not positively embraced, or the trine has been a source of abuse, these aspects will be reversed back to whatever arduous aspect they previously symbolized (such as a square) in a previous incarnation; and displayed as a square once again in the natal chart of a future incarnation. Essentially, trines symbolize prolific transmutations.

According to the Akashic Records the karma of missed opportunity is at an all-time high and I therefore have no hesitation in designating this as a developing dis-ease.

Quintiles: Projections of Self-Mastery

Quintiles and bi-quintiles symbolize the soul's evolutionary continuation, because when these aspects show up in the natal chart, it is usually a precursor to the individual's soul being enlightened and highly evolved. Quintiles are also very Neptunian aspects!

Quintiles and bi-quintiles are often found in the natal charts of seers, adepts and wise souls, and they often appear when interceptions are evident. In some cases the quintile will be connected to the ruling planets of the interception, offering a solution to the puzzle of interceptions. The quintile can evoke the hidden potential of the interception and indicate that the individual has volunteered to return to incarnation when the spiritual soul has agreed to be absolved from the effects of the Earth plane. Quintiles are also predominant healing aspects (refer to Chapter 7 for more information).

Similar to the trine, quintiles and bi-quintiles need to be activated, otherwise they can lead to stagnation. To release the positive energy of the quintile group, the obstacles posed by Saturn in the natal chart must be overcome completely. This is especially important for the highly evolved soul because Saturn literally holds to task without reprieve those intercepted quintile souls who chose to return in order to raise awareness.

In order for the positive expression of the quintile to be embraced, wholly new foundations must be constructed (Saturn). Quintiles and bi-quintiles are Moon-related aspects, and Saturn is the polarity planet of the Moon. When activated, quintiles and bi-quintiles are cultivating aspects that foster the sections of the natal chart that they influence.

A good example of the soul-orientated quintile/bi-quintile is one that would involve the presence of Jupiter, or a luminary, or the outer planets aspected to the Ascendant, or the Part of Fortune. Here Jupiter's benign influence is extremely beneficial and his energy a harbinger for soul ascension, similar to the Sun and the Moon. A Jupiter configuration of this magnitude necessitates a journey of self-discovery attained through the wisdom attached to creative experiences. I am speaking here merely from an esoteric point of view of course.

Along with its benefic twin Venus, and the Moon, Jupiter is a planet of safety, protecting the soul from imminent danger. Quintiles and bi-quintiles also exhibit this effect; they are aspects that help to bolster faith. When identified in the natal chart quintiles denote an individual with a strong immune system able to overcome some of the most prolific illnesses and diseases, especially when Mars, Saturn and Pluto configure in the quintile.

In my opinion, the distinct lack of faith that is evident in the world today must surely be designated as a developing dis-ease simply because it is on the increase. Carl Yung, the Swiss psychiatrist and psychoanalyst said that "twenty-first century human beings will be spiritual, or they won't be spiritual at all."

Developing Dis-eases

They were wise words spoken by Carl Jung! But perhaps the noticeable lack of faith now evident in the majority of the populace is due to a desire to ignore the divine, and instead worship those false deities set in stone in the material world. Worshipping the wrong type of deity is a concerning problem, and one that is now a developing dis-ease, brought to the forefront by the Saturn-Neptune square of 2016.

Increasing levels of self-centerdness coupled with a distinct lack of unique creativity is directly responsible for a large percentage of the world's mental health conditions prevalent throughout the world today. This is why dementia, for example, is on the increase. Dementia (a degenerative and progressive mental health concern) signifies an overall stagnation of creativity that ultimately impacts crucial parts of the brain, such as the hippo campus (the center of the short-term memory that has the Moon as its planetary rulership).

Recently, mental health has been pronounced by the World Health Organisation as a major health concern reaching epic global proportions. The UK government announced that it is seeking to recruit a further 20,000 health specialists by 2020 to help deal with this growing crises, a befitting testament perhaps to the eventual onset of the generational Neptune-Pluto sextile? A wide range of mental health concerns like dementia and depression, with the inclusion of diabetes have been thoroughly investigated and examined throughout this book. Diabetes begins as a mental/eating disorder.

Dementia

Alzheimer's dementia[7] is considered to be one of the redeveloping mental health infirmities of the twenty-first century, reaching monumental proportions. Dementia is a very Neptunian dis-ease because it signifies the dissolving of the short-term memory. I use the word "redeveloping" because dementia has, for centuries, existed in one form or another. Dementia was particularly widespread throughout the medieval period when it was simply referred to as mental decline.

Not only should dementia be designated as a developing dis-ease, it should most definitely be categorised as a tumultuous and unfortunate condition that erodes life experiences. It is equally important that dementia in its harshest form should not merely be perceived as irrelevant and unimportant. In some countries, particularly the UK, the effects of this dis-ease are still not fully understood nor the consequences left by it. There is also a certain amount of stigma attached to dementia; for example, I have even heard it said that to lose one's short term-memory is a sin.

Dementia is a bi-product created mostly by unprecedented thought patterns that typify the concept of hopelessness and inequality. Dementia is often diagnosed during Mercury retrograde cycles. On at least six occasions I have known of certain individuals being diagnosed during Mercury retrograde cycles.

Hopelessness, caused primarily by Mercury's polarity planet, Jupiter, is the psychological trigger to this condition, as it is with so many mental health conditions. In maturity, hopelessness is linked to a psychological refusal to accept the world for how it is, hence a lack of visible direction (Jupiter). The individual who succumbs to the unfortunate effects of dementia exemplifies this condition further by projecting concepts of hopelessness such as: "it wasn't like this in my day." It highlights a refusal to move on in life, and symbolizes ultimate stagnation.

Dementia sufferers instinctively blot out the everyday realities of their often uncomfortable and unacceptable circumstances (a Neptune trait that we will examine further on), preferring instead to live in the past, because to them the past (a projection of the long-term memory) remains safe and familiar territory—the precept of dementia.

Dementia is a dis-ease that is often accentuated by the effects of the Moon-Saturn polarity in the natal chart. In addition, dementia occurs when transiting Neptune aspects the natal Moon or Ascendant, either by square or opposition. If a transit like this occurs in later life then it may mean that Neptune's purpose is readying the individual for its preparation to the spirit realms.

However, when the soul departs onwards for the spirit world having already contracted dementia, ultimately it will be completely unaware of this extraordinary transition — transcending it partway back to its true home. Is this what was meant by dementia being a sin I wonder? Meanwhile, the concept of sin has always been designated a developing dis-ease.

Depression

The illusion of martyrdom is misconceived as reality when the individual succumbs to the terrifying influence of depression.

Saturn is the main catalyst for depression; and depression is the foundation stone for virtually, if not all, of the mental health afflictions in existence today. Depression is a developing dis-ease, continuing to develop through the chasm of time (the centuries). The effects from depression will reach a pinnacle in the 21st century at the culmination of the Saturn/Pluto conjunction in 2020, at which point I estimate it will become a global epidemic.

Both Saturn and Mars suppress the release of endorphins to the brain under the influence of heavy arduous transits. Endorphins are endogenous opioid neuropeptides produced by the central nervous system and the pituitary gland (ruled by Jupiter). Suppressing the natural flow of endorphins to the brain can lead to the onset of depression because endorphins are the optimism impulses (Jupiter), whereas Saturn is known for his gloomy disposition.

Also, the consumption of contaminated water is a trigger for depression, allow me to explain. Saturn rules the body's calcium deposits, and particularly those contained and compressed within the spinal column. The main purpose of the spinal column, aside from supporting the body, is to compact the central nervous system and underpin the chakras. In addition, Saturn acts as a kind of arterial root canal that delivers water directly to the brain.

Calcium deposits, along with potassium (a Moon-ruled mineral see Chapter 7) pervade the natural essence of water. Because of the tumultuous levels of destruction and pollution inflicted on the Earth over the last two thousand years or so, and now leaving a venomous residue at the outgoing Piscean Age, Saturn is delivering mostly polluted water directly to the brain. And this water is devoid of all the essential nutrients, including calcium and potassium. The lack of calcium and potassium in the diet leads to the onset of depression.

This is another reason why Saturn's energy is considered difficult to work with, because its influence is contaminated. The ancients referred to Saturn as the great spiritual healer. I believe that notion to be long-since dead.

Today, the effects of illness and disease, especially dementia and depression, will only accelerate as the Earth becomes increasingly polluted.

Healing

In order to prevent dementia and depression I recommend healthy and sustainable nutrition, particularly increased amounts of calcium and potassium for depression (see Chapter 10). Only drink clean unpolluted water, preferably distilled or glacial water. Remember to infuse distilled water with nutrients such as Himalayan pink rock salt.

Developing dis-eases must be completely eliminated before healing can ultimately occur—individually and collectively.

Chart Data

Foundation chart for the World Health Organisation, April 7. 1948, 12: 00 Noon, Geneva, Switzerland. Placidus house, mean Node.

UK Sibley chart, December 25, 1066, 12:00 Noon, Westminster, UK. Placidus houses, mean Node.

Susan Boyle, April 1, 1961, 9:50 AM, Blackburn, West Lothian, Scotland. Placidus system, mean Node.

Susan Boyle wins talent show, April 11, 2009, 6:00 PM, London, England. Placidus system, mean Node.

Susan Boyle breakdown Heathrow Airport, April 26, 2016, 12:00 noon, London, England. Placidus system, mean Node.

Oscar Pistorius, November 22, 1986, 10:30 AM, Johannesburg, South Africa. Placidus house, mean Node.

Endnotes

[1] Reported in the *Times* newspaper, June 17, 2017.

[2] Information Source *Wikipedia*

[3] According to Kushal Kumar (a Vedic astrologer) the Part of Fortune becomes less *fortunate* when applied to the quincunx.

[4] Information source "The Journal of a Fallen Angel" by the newspaper journalist Max Hastings.

[5] Information source *The Sunday Mirror* newspaper.

[6] Anaretic is a term used for a "deficient" degree.

[7] The symptoms of this dis-ease were first identified by *Emil Kraepelin*, and the characteristic was first observed by *Alois Alzheimer* in 1906. Despite modern-day consensus the seer *Edgar Cayce* believed Alzheimer's disease and dementia are different expressions of the same disease.

Part Two
Prognosis

"No patient can possibly be cured by the industry of his physician, be he never so learned, without the benevolent configuration of the stars."—William Lilly

Chapter Four

The Counterpoint Effect

> "The purpose of astrology is to work constructively with the influences of the cosmos that will help us to take control of our own spiritual destiny."—Barbara Marciniak

Disclaimer: All persons whose cases and charts are discussed and illustrated in this chapter gave their permission to disclose the relevant details—excluding Glen Campbell whose birth details are widely available on various websites including *Astrotheme*.

Hitherto, when I was compiling my first book *One Body Many Illnesses: An Insightful Approach to Medical Astrology*, my attention was instinctively drawn to the Moon's polarized Nodes. I found myself being pressed into appraising the impact these pivotal points have upon the natal chart, especially when scrutinizing them from an evolutionary and medical perspective.

Furthermore, I found myself asking the hierarchal intelligence an important question do these points upon the ecliptic and their planetary rulers display any connection to illness and disease? The answer I received via my meditations was "*Yes*, they most definitely do, and they should not be overlooked when interpreting the chart." Therefore, the Nodal polarities and their symbolic planetary rulerships—drawing out their connection to illness—became the main focus of this first major publication.

After determining that the Nodes and their rulership planets are lynchpins and starting points for medical analysis, I was able to devise an alternate and accurate form of chart diagnosis to ascertain the likelihood and potential onset of illness and disease, as shown in the many case studies throughout the book. I refer to this proven formula as: *Lunar Nodal Connections*.[1]

Karmic Illness

Illness and disease that is karmic by definition is often a reoccurring factor prevalent throughout the lives of countless souls. Allow me to explain! Encased within the mainstream of the general consciousness, an individual retains the vibration of karmic illness, encompassing it within the aural soul energy field. For the most part, an individual's current path of incarnation resonates at a similar vibration to a life that has already been lived—generations past.

Henceforth the cycle of incarnation has a repeating echo of faint unimpressive undertones pointing to a life of stasis. In essence, a static echo means that the soul, at some point, has endured an Earth life absent of any spiritual progression. Therefore, the continuation of a life of stasis in the here and now becomes a trigger for karmic illness and disease.

In some cases however, this karmic reverberation bellows the potential for evolutionary growth. But for the majority of the time, the earthen tapestries that signify past lives are bound together with the karmic threads of illness and disease, and are thus projected into the here and now. Meanwhile, the pitfalls and the positive qualities displayed in a past life are highlighted by the Moon's Nodes.

When an illness or disease is termed congenital, it confirms that the soul has endured a similar trauma in a past life and is playing it out again. Congenital illness particularly afflicts souls who are strongly connected to generational family groups (souls who refuse to break the attachment after the death of a loved one); and, as previously touched upon, congenital illness will afflict unconscious souls who have lived out previous incarnations existing merely in stasis. In other words, living a life where a complete lack of spiritual progression, awareness and faith are abundant.

At the heart centre we are all spiritual beings. According to the Akashic Records humankind represent the angelic children of the angelic host. This is a universal axiom that remains constant whether we chose to acknowledge it or not. However, it is a difficult concept to comprehend, especially in light of the increasing negativity in the world. When a life has been lived in stasis or stagnation it is deemed throughout the spirit world as *purgatory*, and congenital illness is a form of purgatory. In most cases when the soul is being called back to the spirit world, death means *death* and not *transformation*.

Identifying the Stasis Chart

Stasis charts are easy to identify because to the competent astrologer they pose merely as uninteresting. In most cases, stasis charts are void of evolutionary markers such as tense aspects like squares and oppositions, quintiles and intercepted houses and planets. Stasis charts often display an abundance of soft aspects and fewer frictional aspects, projecting a distinct lack of strength and sturdiness. When under the influence of a challenging life cycle the individual might simply fall apart and be overwhelmed with emotion, unable to cope with the pressing situation.

Karmic illness such as cancer is emphasized in the natal chart when there is an abundance of *hard* conjunctions (see further on).

The South Node

It is imperative at this stage to highlight the importance of the South Node, its planetary ruler, the segment positions in the chart, and the aspects, paying particular attention to conjunctions. It is equally important to stipulate that if we fail to evoke the positive effects governed by this point, its influence will continue to reoccur at a negative and karmic level. Medically speaking, the purpose of the North Node is to expunge the concept of karmic illness.

Initially the South Node determines whether a karmic illness or disease is likely to reoccur, especially if the illness or disease was responsible for the termination of the life in a previous incarnation. Therefore, if the individual's life was derailed or even wiped out by cancer, there is a strong possibility that the cancer will become a possibility once again, especially if either Node is afflicted. This is because the nucleus of the disease will be contained in the South Node and will be projected via the North Node—which symbolizes the current incarnation. The planetary rulers of the Nodes aid the healing process if and when the illness goes into successful remission.

However, it is important to point out that illness and disease do not necessarily occur in the same format. For example, if cancer was responsible for the termination of life, and if the South Node tenants the sign of Taurus, the chances are the cancer would have started in the area of the throat. In this example we could surmise that a life was terminated by oesophageal cancer, or that cancer may have affected the vocal chords—perhaps rendering the victim speechless, especially if the South Node tenants the third house. If the cancer returns in the current life it is possible that it manifests in the bowel or reproductive regions because in this example the North Node tenants the sign of Scorpio.

An important point to remember is that the duration of the cancer from the point of diagnosis to the outcome will occur for the same period of time as it did previously. Remember if the soul refuses to acknowledge the presence of the North Node everything will play out exactly as previously. Furthermore, if the cancer is diagnosed as being *congenital*, examine the house position and aspects to the South Node to acquire an accurate analysis that the illness or disease is in fact reoccurring. An admissible dispositor to this notion is if the Nodes occupy succedent (fixed) houses. Also, the positions of Saturn and Pluto and Mars as the trigger and the aspects in the natal chart should provide a further indication as to whether a congenital illness or disease is likely to reoccur.

Further analysis of conjunctions (see further on) to the South Node or its ruler should also stand out as a clear detection of that karmic signature; especially if the South Node or its ruler is besieged by other planets, particularly by those aforementioned. This is why the Nodes and the planetary rulers are karmic geometric pointers that possess hidden messages that can determine illness and disease in the natal chart, particularly during the presence of difficult transitory cycles.

It is worth reiterating that astrology is an excellent tool that raises awareness to the karma that envelopes the soul; and once awareness has been raised and acknowledged healing can begin.

The Counterpoint Effect

Now, I would like to propose an additional hypothesis and one that further highlights the potential for the onset of karmic illness and disease in the natal and especially the decumbiture chart. In this example, the lynchpin or the starting point is incurred within an intense mergence of planetary interplay, which is evident at the time of diagnosis, though in most cases unforeseen. In effect, this new supposition shares the same values as Lunar Nodal Connections, especially when transiting planets conjoin the Nodes and their planetary rulers.

Aptly named, I refer to this as the Counterpoint Effect. But what exactly is a Counterpoint? According to *Wikipedia* a Counterpoint is 'a melodious part of a symphony,' hence the combination of parts that accompany a musical melody. In this respect, the Counterpoint Effect is merely a fanciful title I have designated to the powerful and underlying conjunction. To be more precise, the Counterpoint Effect recognizes the conjunction as the starting point for the diagnosis of illness. The conjunction is an essential part of medical diagnosis because similar to its twin aspect the opposition, the conjunction represents a dichotomy of influence and combined ideals that are in need of synthesizing.

With that said, let us continue with this musical theme with regards to the conjunction and medical diagnosis that characterizes the Counterpoint Effect.

A Collaboration of Musical Melodies

Musically speaking, the conjunction symbolizes a harmonic resonance field that is comprised solely of unified sound waves and dialogues that ultimately reach a crescendo, or the point of exactitude. At the point of exactitude they merge to become the final synchronous melody—some of which are harmonious, others are more challenging, yet each plays out in its own unique and influential mode of resonance.

For the most part, the final melody is synchronized during the first degree of planetary separation of the conjunction. This denotes the purpose of the aspect and highlights a physical, emotional or mental imbalance. The conjunction will also produce an opportunity for growth and spiritual transformation, depending on the planets concerned. The sound wave harmonics that determine the frequency of the melody are always configured by its geometric equation (the specific degree of the planets) that resonates on the entire zodiac—comprised of course of the twelve signs.

So, for example, if the Counterpoint Effect forms at eight degrees of any sign, this Uranian degree will denote the potential for an accident.[2] Therefore, caution must always be applied.

First Degree of Separation/Application

The point that is referred to as the first degree of separation, denotes a transitory aspect only—a transiting planet to a natal planet. However, if the Counterpoint (conjunction) occurs solely between natal planets then the final degree of application is applied, specifying the flexibility of the Counterpoint Effect once more. In my opinion, both the first degree of application and the first degree of separation are representative of the Counterpoint Effect. Musically speaking, this multiple band- width cosmic transmission emits the highest frequency of sound resonance, from the base tones of the applying Counterpoint to the base-soprano tones of the Counterpoint's first degree of separation.

The Counterpoint Effect represents the most poignant, potent and pivotal point of any planetary aspectual configuration. The Counterpoint Effect denotes both the one degree arc of application and separation and determines the most intense point of color synonymous of the aspect (see Chapter 12, Guided Meditations, for a list of aspectual colour coordinations).

In my previous publication, *One Body Many Illnesses*, I brought to the forefront the Moon's biorhythms and their significant connection to astrology. I conveyed how illness and disease can occur during periods of biorhythm depletion. Interestingly, when the Counterpoint Effect is located in the natal chart or decumbiture chart it will also indicate biorhythm depletion, especially during the first degree of separation. It would however be wise to check the primary biorhythms during periods when the Counterpoint Effect is evident in the horoscope when transiting planets are in effect, especially if squares are involved.

Also, during periods when the Counterpoint Effect is evident, it is equally important to consume additional vitamin and mineral supplements, as the body leaches essential nutrients during planetary cycles when the one degree arc of application/separation is in effect. For more information about vitamin and mineral deficiency in the natal chart refer to Chapter 10.

Finally, to conclude this information, once the first degree arc of separation culminates, the waning effect begins, and the aspect's harmonic resonance starts toning down, gradually drawing to its cosmic conclusion. This effect can be likened to the slow movement of a three-part orchestral symphony.

Aspectual Effects

In order to put the Counterpoint Effect to the test, let us briefly examine a typical stationary (natal) aspect such as a Venus-Saturn opposition or square (traditionally speaking this can be likened to a Fortune meeting an Infortune, or a Sympathy meeting an Antipathy according to William Lilly). During the one degree arc of separation, or in this case the last degree of application, Sympathy's and Antipathy's are at their most effective in both cases. It can often be determined at this point whether the symptoms of the disease are deemed chronic or acute. Acute symptoms can often be caused by the application of the Counterpoint, whereas chronic symptoms can often be caused by the separation of the Counterpoint Effect.

In this Counterpoint example, let us presume that Saturn resides at twelve degrees four minutes of Aries (detrimental). Therefore, in order for this aspect to reach its separating Counterpoint, Venus would have to station at twelve degrees five minutes of Libra (dignified) moving to an orb of influence denoting thirteen degrees and five minutes of Libra. Alternatively, in the case of application Venus would have to be stationed at eleven degrees four minutes of Libra, moving towards and reaching its point of exactitude respectively.

Likewise, a Venus/Libra-Saturn/Capricorn square, as shown in the natal chart 1 example, would be interpreted in exactly the same way. Here, both planets are dignified, so the effects of any occurring illness or disease would naturally be personified. However, in this natal example of a former client (see natal chart), Venus and Saturn have *not* reached their Counterpoint.

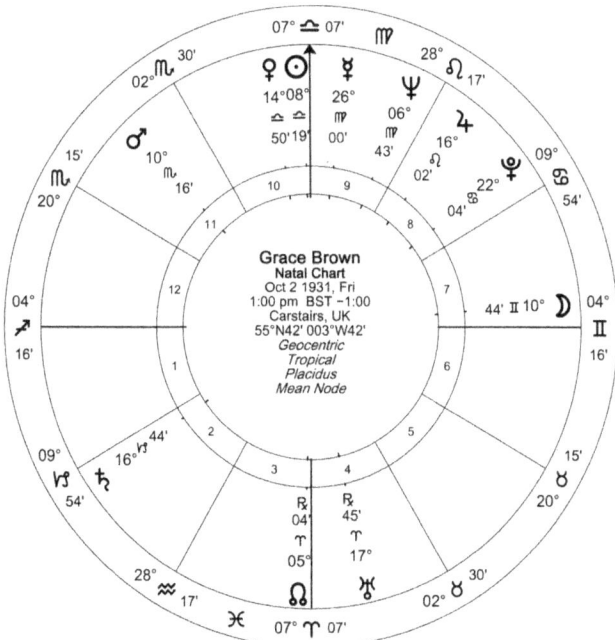

Diagnosis: Kidney Stones

A common and likely scenario to occur under the influence of the Venus-Saturn opposition-square is kidney stones, exemplifying Saturn's hardening effect over the Venus-Libra rulership of the kidneys. Generally speaking, kidney stones are designated as neither illness nor disease and merely categorised as a physical dis-ease with the potential for infection. According to Louise Hay, kidney stones are extreme forms of concentrated anger.

Meanwhile, under the influence of a Venus-Saturn opposition-square, kidney stones would no doubt become a potential hazard in later life. A Venus-Saturn opposition-square would indicate the gradual formation of calcium deposits in the kidneys that would come to light when triggered by the presence of a heavy transit especially of Mars, Saturn or Pluto, which have also reached their Counterpoint (see decumbiture chart above). There would be complications to this condition if the Venus-

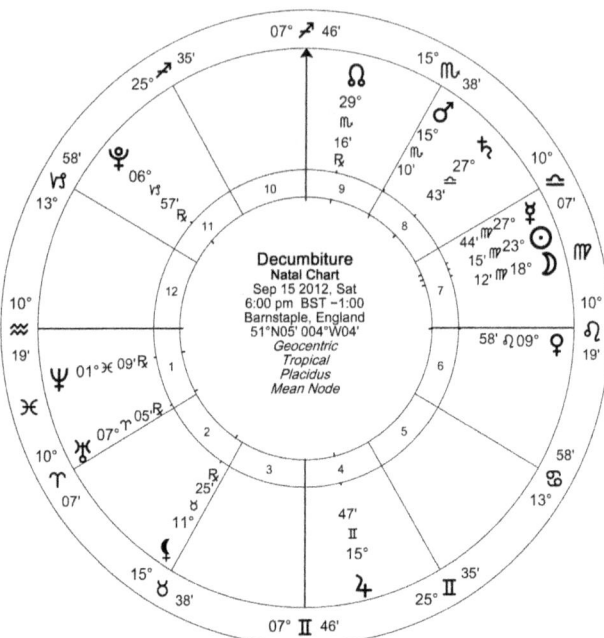

Saturn opposition-square had reached its Counterpoint during the time of birth.

Alternative Treatments

The visualization of purple and crimson red light during breath meditation, will over a period of time successfully alleviate kidney stones, as an alternative spiritual remedy. In addition, as a physical remedy, I would recommend high doses of perfectly-coordinated multivitamins coupled with sea kelp and the omega fatty acids—preferably in krill oil form (because krill oil doesn't absorb the high levels of mercury concentrates currently polluting many of Earth's oceans and seas). If kidney stones have grown to exceptional proportions then laser treatment would also be recommended.

For vegetarians and vegans, omegas 3, 6 and 9 found in plant sterols can also be used as an alternative to the fish variety, or alternatively for those souls who show an innate sensitivity to krill oil. This can often be the case when the Ascendant, Moon, Neptune and Pluto are afflicted in the horoscope. Regular consumption of organic asparagus (Libra ruled) will also help to neutralize the presence of kidney stones over a period of time.

Progressions and transits are interpreted in exactly the same way as natal Counterpoints, confirming once again that the diagnosis of illness and disease can also be successfully attributed to the proposed Counterpoint Effect.

Prognosis

Applying an additional examination to the kidney stone decumbiture chart 2 here, we can see that at the time of kidney stone diagnosis transiting Mars had reached its Counterpoint at 15 degrees of Libra forming a conjunction with natal Venus and impacting on Saturn. Pluto was also influencing the Venus-Saturn square. This one element was, in my opinion, enough to warrant the formation of kidney stones.

Of course there are always many more significators to be taken into consideration when exemplifying the importance of Counterpoints, which will be touched upon throughout the various celebrity case studies in Chapter 7.

This particular chapter however serves merely as a guide to emphasise the notability and relevance of the all-important Counterpoint and to highlight its effects through several case examples beginning with: Borderline Personality Disorder.

Borderline Personality Disorder

Before I use the Counterpoint Effect to examine in detail the predicament of a well known celebrity figure, Glen Campbell, who unfortunately succumbed to the effects of Alzheimer's dementia, I wish to present three further examples of lesser-known individuals who have all succumbed to the effects of dis-eases only recently categorised under the Mental Health Act. The pur-

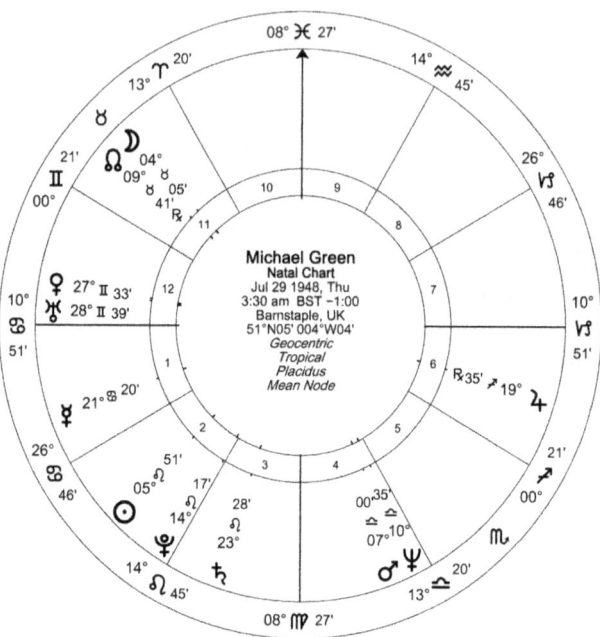

pose of which will emphasize once again the significance of the Counterpoint Effect in natal and decumbiture chart analysis and diagnosis.

Similar to a significant number of mental health conditions, Borderline Personality Disorder (BPD)[3], and an apparent form of schizophrenia according to the World Health Organisation (WHO), emanates, it is believed, from the effects of manic depression.

Displayed in the natal chart is a single Counterpoint that points categorically to this genetic mental health condition. Here we can easily identify the catalyst for this condition as a tight conjunction between Venus and Uranus at their Counterpoint—signifying sudden and intermittent changes (Uranus) within the personality (Venus) that occur at irregular intervals. Often these personality shifts can manifest as highly-charged

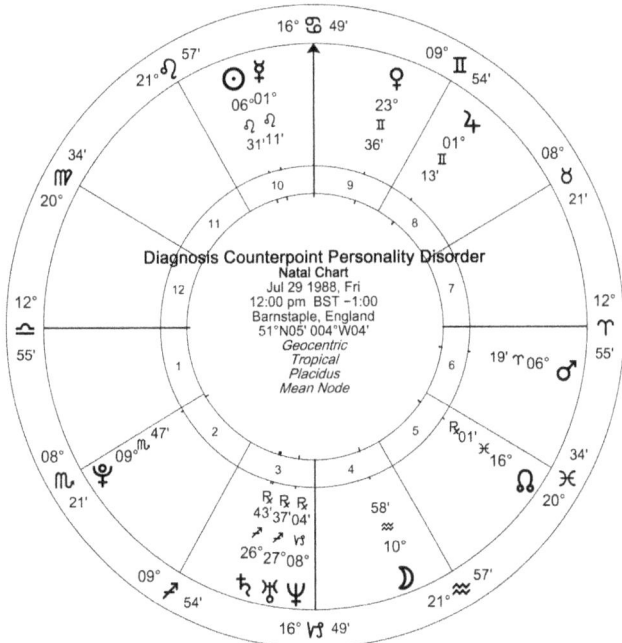

emotional outbursts (Uranus in the twelfth house). Gemini, the sign the planets tenant, exacerbates the situation because Gemini frequently demonstrates a preference towards mental duality and emotional confusion. Before healing can successfully take place this particular conjunction needs to be grounded.

Michael Green (a former client) was diagnosed with Borderline Personality Disorder on July 29, 1988 (see chart on next page). Without going into too much detail here perhaps the most striking feature of this decumbiture chart is the close conjunction between Saturn and Uranus directly opposing the Venus/Uranus Counterpoint in the natal chart at the time of diagnosis. After a careful and stringent prognosis, clearly this would indicate the catalyst for the onset of Borderline Personality Disorder. I would also consider this particular client to be on the spectrum bordering between insanity and normality.

Astrology for Self-Healing   83

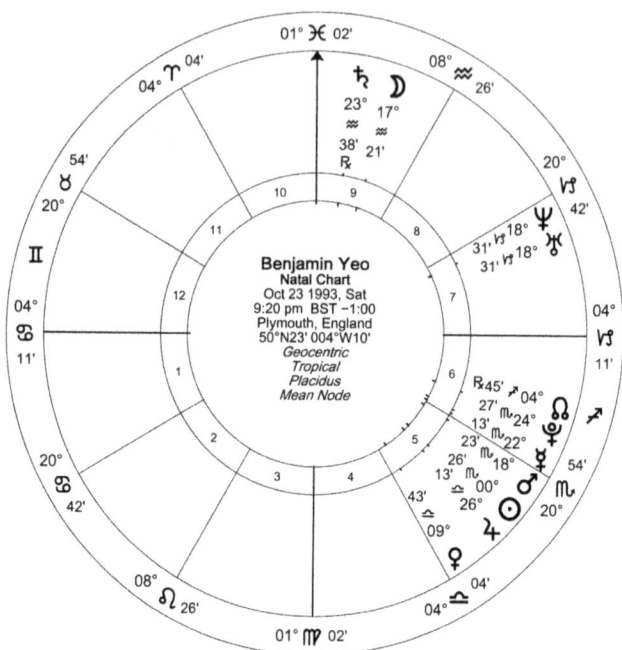

Attention Deficit Hyperactive Disorder

There are many other mental health issues and conditions that are triggered and brought into manifestation when psychological snags impose upon the spirituality of the individual. Impositions such as the overcrowding or stifling of the personality causing a lack of mental and psychological growth, and/or a deliberate invasion of the individual's privacy by imposing sanctions. In other words, "Don't think you are going to do that until you finish that"—kind of thing.

These unfortunate encumbrances are often relevant and consistent during the diagnosis and onset of the disturbing dis-ease called Attention Deficit Hyperactive Disorder, or ADHD as it is more commonly referred to. Now designated by the World Health Organisation as a condition paralleling Borderline Personality Disorder this modern-day mental dysfunction is on the increase, especially throughout western civilization and specifically amongst teenagers. (Although it must be stressed that ADHD is not a dis-ease that affects children). Recently, it has been confirmed by the World Health Organisation that ADHD also occurs in adults particularly over forty years of age. Medication, as opposed to more effective measures such as psychotherapy or hypnotherapy, is still the preferred prognosis where alternative therapies are considered irrelevant. Thus, medication for this ailment is still prevalent in the United Kingdom, where, surprising as it may seem, very little is actually known about this borderline condition.

ADHD is often diagnosed when natal Saturn and Neptune conjoin or make hard aspects to the Sun, the Moon, Mercury or Uranus in the natal chart, as intricately displayed in this particular example, see natal chart 5. What is striking about this chart is the wide conjunction with the Moon and Saturn both squared to Mercury (domiciled), Mars (dignified) and Pluto (dignified). Mercury is also besieged. Perhaps the most interesting factor is the applying Counterpoint between Uranus and Neptune, which inevitably would be the catalyst for ADHD. Neptune is also debilitated in Capricorn (in its fall). Saturn and Uranus are also in mutual reception. These planetary refractions would subsequently increase the effects of the dis-ease ADHD.

Interestingly, the emotional outbursts that are associated with ADHD are consistently brought about when these planetary patterns involving Saturn and Neptune are triggered by the Moon—particularly at the time of the Full Moon cycles and eclipses.

This individual frequently complained about his difficulties with sleeping, and the Uranus-Neptune Counterpoint would no doubt be the cause of this problem (see Chapter 9, Sleep Deprivation, for further information).

A Case of Epilepsy

According to the World Health Organisation (WHO) epilepsy is on the increase. Epileptic type seizures are also connected to the disorder meningitis: a viral infection of the protective membranes that surround the brain and spinal cord. Meningitis is also on the increase according to WHO. Statistics suggest that these vexatious dis-eases have multiplied in the last 50 years. Today it is thought that approximately 2 in 10 of the overall global population suffer from one of these conditions.

In the natal chart of a client (an epilepsy sufferer who preferred not to have their personal details disclosed) is a powerful quincunx between domiciled Mercury in Gemini and an exalted Uranus in Scorpio. The quincunx is in my opinion the main catalyst for the onset of this dreadful dis-ease. Mercury is also semi-sextiled to an afflicted Mars in Cancer (in its fall). Mercury symbolizes the conventional brainwave patterns of the left brain (logic), whereas Uranus symbolizes the higher brainwave patterns of the right brain (intuition). At the time the epilepsy was first diagnosed transit Saturn conjoined Uranus within one degree, hence at an applying Counterpoint, and therefore forming another quincunx to domicile Mercury. Progressed Mars was also opposing Uranus.

Cerebral Convulsions

Epilepsy can be likened to a palpitating quake (Uranus) in the brain, where the left and right brain somehow collide with each other; similar to the Earth's tectonic plates applying pressure against each other and not dissimilar to the Counterpoint Effect. So, perhaps it would be apt to say that the convulsions linked to epilepsy are in essence a kind of brainquake taking place.

Magnesium, selenium, zinc, iodine and flax seed oil taken as food supplements are recommended to alleviate the effects of epilepsy. Also, calcium Pantothenate (vitamin B5) is recommended to counteract the effects associated with epilepsy. I

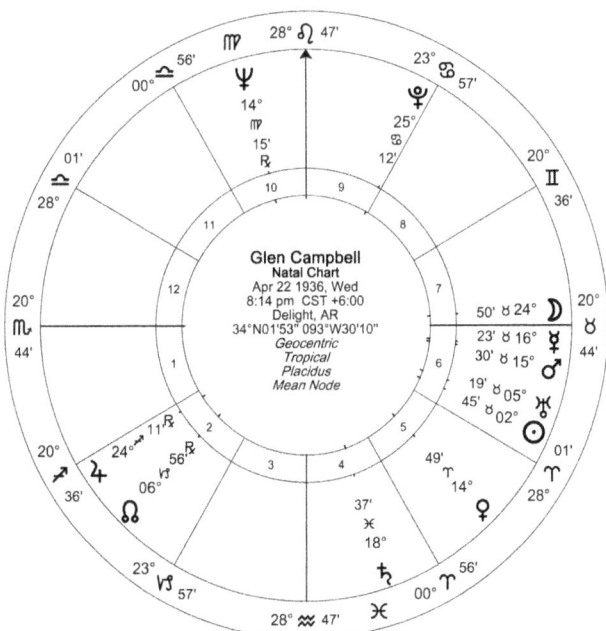

would also recommend breath meditation to help alleviate the potential side-effects and dangers associated with conventional medications. At the spiritual level epilepsy occurs when the body lacks cohesion, peace, harmony and tranquillity. Now let us examine the chart of the singer Glen Campbell for the cause of his dementia.

Glen Campbell

In June 2011 the popular country and western singer Glen Campbell announced that he had been diagnosed with Alzheimer's dementia; although he had in fact been officially diagnosed with this condition in January 2011. However, he had been aware that his health had begun to deteriorate possibly from dementia much earlier than 2011—indeed several years earlier to be precise. The actual timeframe of his deteriorating health is unknown, but what is known is that some form of misdiagnosis occurred long before he was officially diagnosed with dementia.

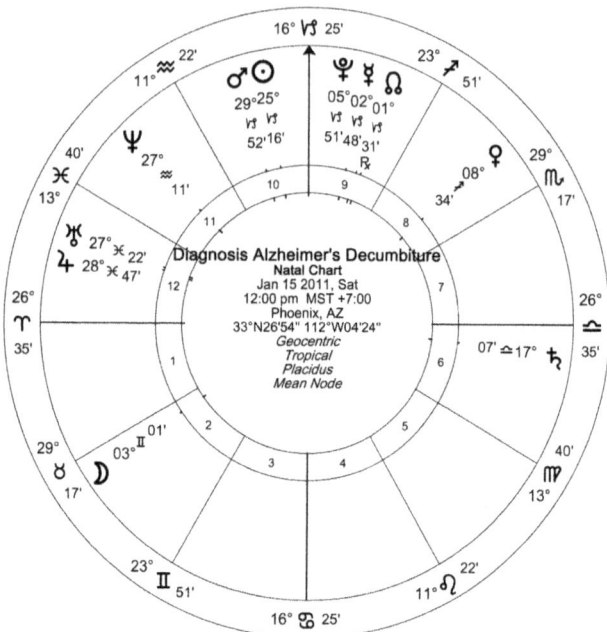

In other words he was told that dementia wasn't suspected at that time.[4]

Dementia, like so many other mental health issues, signifies an inauspicious end to life, particularly if the disease is viral. In most cases, dementia isn't the immediate cause of death; death is often brought about by the side-effects of this disease such as pneumonia. Regrettably, dementia is the catalyst that destroyed the life of an entertainer who brought pleasure to millions of people all over the world through his upbeat and sensual ballad-type songs. But Glen Campbell is yet another superstar celebrity who found it increasingly difficult to cope with the pressures of stardom—an illusion that many would perceive as a preferred lifestyle.

Addictions

Over the course of several years Glen Campbell struggled to curb an alcohol and cocaine addiction that began in the 1970s.

Quite likely, this was the result of Saturn's opposition to a debilitated Neptune in his natal chart (see chart)—Saturn tenanting Neptune's sign of Pisces. This configuration was perhaps also responsible for his inability to cope with fame and stature. Throughout the course of the 1970s, transit Neptune in Sagittarius joined with the Saturn-Neptune opposition as the apex planet of a t-square. The formation of this powerful pattern could have marked the beginning of his alcohol and drug problem. In addition, transit Neptune formed an antagonistic quincunx aspect to the Mercury/Mars Counterpoint, giving nuance to an already critical situation.

At the midpoint of the Saturn-Neptune natal opposition is Jupiter domiciled in Sagittarius. Ordinarily, this additional influence would have multiplied his need for artificial stimulants as a way of making the journey bearable. Campbell had obviously reached a crises point in his life. Also, hazy Neptune is exactly quincunx a debilitated Venus in the natal chart bringing further imbalance and adding insult to injury. Furthermore, Neptune's trine to the Mercury/Mars connection may have suggested that he had in fact developed a talent and one that outlined the frequent misuse of alcohol and drugs.

Sleep Deprivation

Sources close to him also suggested that he had suffered from years of sleep deprivation (for further clarification to the causes of sleep disorders refer to Chapter 9: Sleep Deprivation). In fact his wife Kim (Kimberley) told the newspapers in a series of interviews that "my husband never slept when he was on tour."[5] Examined in depth in Chapter 9 sleep deprivation occurs when either the Moon or Neptune (glamour and music) are afflicted in the natal chart. This being the case Neptune's opposition to Saturn and the Moon's dignified opposition to the Ascendant and its quincunx to Jupiter are likely to be the main catalysts for his ongoing sleep deprivation.

Glen Campbell and the Counterpoint Effect

Examining the natal chart of Glen Campbell further (see chart), we can easily identify two planets positioned at their Counterpoint, as previously indicated. Mercury and Mars are within one degree of a separating conjunction, and also receive a discordant sextile from Saturn. The Mercury-Mars Counterpoint opposes the Ascendant. So, because of Mercury's input here, does it mean that a type of mental illness is likely and would affect him in later life? Certainly it is a distinct possibility.

When Glen Campbell was diagnosed with Alzheimer's dementia on the January 15, 2011 (see chart, left) a Counterpoint had formed between transit Jupiter and Uranus, which had previously impacted on the Saturn/Neptune opposition in his natal chart. This would have played a major part in the diagnosis of this disease and would also have highlighted any potential misdiagnosis that occurred prior to January 2011, as the sign of the transit Counterpoint is Pisces—even the twelfth house of Neptune features.

The Mercury-Mars conjunction suggests that he was prone to mineral deficiency, particularly lecithin and selenium, essential minerals for the prevention of cognitive diseases such as dementia (see Chapter 10 for a list of vitamins and minerals). And Saturn's connection to the Counterpoint and its opposition to Neptune would also determine that his vitamin C levels were constantly depleted, mainly due to the alcohol and cocaine abuse.

A further significant point to raise is when Mercury rises in the first house or opposes the Ascendant from the domicile health-orientated sixth house, the messenger can act as a trigger for ensuing mental health problems. The likelihood is that Saturn's influence on the Mercury/Mars Counterpoint was problematic and when combined they were a major contributor for the onset of dementia.[6]

Although sextiles are generally considered to be harmonious aspects denoting the prospect of opportunity, the Saturn inevitability via the sextile was to solidify the likelihood of dementia at the time of diagnosis, mainly because of the pitiless influence of Mercury and Mars opposing the Ascendant in the natal chart. In addition, Saturn's effects are naturally multiplied from the angular fourth house in Jupiter's traditional rulership sign. If diagnosis really did take place, as suggested, much earlier than January 2011, then transit Neptune's square to the Mercury-Mars Counterpoint could very well have been the additional catalyst for the onset of dementia—especially when it was originally misdiagnosed. Moreover, at the time of the initial diagnosis, transit Neptune was tenanting Aquarius, ruled by Uranus, a planet also associated with mental health problems—Uranus being the other half of the transit Counterpoint.

At the time of the January 2011 diagnosis, the transiting South Node made a semi-square to the Mercury/Mars Counterpoint (see chart 7), perhaps denoting the illness had karmic implications. Also, an exalted Saturn applies itself to the Counterpoint with an antagonistic quincunx; and quincunxes are often concerned with poor health, even death. (For an in-depth analysis on the quincunx refer to Chapter 3, Developing Dis-eases).

Finally, at the time of compiling this in-depth analysis (December 2016) Glen Campbell's dementia had reached stage six of the disease. It was also reported at this time that his memory had deteriorated to the point where he no longer recognized his own acoustic guitar.

In Hindsight

If Glen Campbell had not been addicted to alcohol and cocaine I have no doubt that he had the potential to become one of, if not the greatest, singer-songwriters ever to frequent the plane of the Earth. An iconic voice amongst very few others whose persona reflected a beautifully-polished and faceted diamond, as opposed to a mere *Rhinestone*, as his 1975 hit song implied.

Lastly, I would like to point out that when this publication was completed (June 2017) it was reported that Glen Campbell was in the final stages of Alzheimer's dementia. He died August 8, 2017, aged 81.

Conclusion

The two case examples examined in detail here represent the merest fraction of the Counterpoint potential. In my opinion, the Counterpoint Effect can help to simplify medical diagnosis in the natal chart and in the decumbiture chart. My aim here was merely to establish the significance of the Counterpoint Effect, especially when implemented in medical astrology, although this type of interpretation technique can be applied throughout all genres of astrology.

We now know that the Counterpoint Effect occurs when a planetary conjunction is identified as moving to within one degree orb of influence, either applying or separating in this case. And frictional aspects to the Counterpoint increase its potency and potential. The one degree arc of application/separation represents the true condition of the conjunction; and in this case all that it stands for. In my opinion, conjunctions, especially when in Counterpoint mode, are merely pulsations of cosmic potential with regards to healing. Pulsations of cosmic potential become especially relevant when the planets involved in the conjunction or other aspects to it feature those that are traditionally referred to as the Sympathy's and Antipathy's, particularly when trines or quintiles are involved.

Just one final point to mention here, the geometric degree of a planet also has to be taken into consideration because an important degree, such as 8 degrees of a sign signifying potential accidents, will have a further bearing on the conjunction and alter the ecliptic pulsations emitted by the Counterpoint Effect.

And Finally, a Brief Word about Cancer

I have long suspected that in 99 percent of cases cancer forms in the body when bodily cells (Saturn) divide and cause what is termed as "random mistakes." However, what I am about to propose will challenge the widespread opinion that cancer mutations are more often than not considered congenital, or are triggered by environmental factors. My thoughts about cell division have now been endorsed by a handful of scientists, and perhaps more importantly the cell division hypothesis has been endorsed by the World Health Organization.

This doesn't negate the fact that cancer is often congenital. Congenital cancer occurs when strands of DNA (Pluto) somehow become divided at birth causing the aforementioned random errors (Neptune), which ultimately create cell division in the body at some point during the life. This seemingly catastrophic transition occurs because it has happened in a previous life. That is what the word congenital means—that it has occurred before.

Speaking merely from a physical perspective, random errors are likely to occur if the mother consumes large amounts of alcohol, smokes tobacco or cannabis, or ingests drugs, particularly the synthetic drug known as Spice (Neptune), during her nine month term of pregnancy.

It is important to consider here also that Neptune and Pluto rarely work alone. In other words one influences the other and vice versa so to speak. In chart diagnosis Neptune and Pluto should be interpreted as a single synchronized influence. In mythology Neptune and Pluto were actually brothers, and the teachings of esoteric astrology reveal that Pluto was once a moon of Neptune; this is a notion I would strongly endorse!

It is also my belief that cell division occurs when a normal cell divides and copies its DNA to produce two more cells, which can cause cell degeneration, which is what the term "multiple mistake" applies to.

The Conjunction Aspect

This "dividing of the cells ramification theory" is similar to the overall impact of a difficult conjunction aspect. Conjunctions symbolize unification (when a conjunction is applying), especially when Venus is involved. However, they too can signify separation (when a conjunction is separating), especially when Saturn or Pluto is heavily involved. Ultimately, cell division is likely to occur when there are one or more separating conjunctions in the natal chart. For example, if Saturn is highlighted in a separating conjunction in the chart, particularly with Mars, then cell division is a strong possibility.

Alternatively, if Neptune or Pluto are highlighted in a separating conjunction the likelihood that cell division has occurred via the DNA at birth, or sometime after is also a strong possibility. Applied conjunctions in the chart often symbolize the body in the process of healing itself from the effects of a congenital (past life) dis-ease. Cell division is emphasized in the natal chart at the time of diagnosis via the decumbiture chart, especially when there are also conjunctions present, as was the case with Glen Campbell's dementia. Meanwhile, I believe these copying mistakes are a potent source of cancer mutations that have, up to now, been mostly unrecognised and even undervalued.

Therefore, with this in mind I estimate that cancer will increase globally during the Saturn/Pluto Counterpoint, hence the much-publicized and perhaps feared conjunction of 2020. And that said, are we about to witness a global incursion of this deadly and diverse disease? I wonder!

Prevention of Cancer

Consuming the appropriate vitamins and minerals such as vitamin C, D and K, boron and lecithin as part of a healthy diet will help to guard against cell division in the body regardless of the conjunctions. Channelling violet, silver and gold light to the vulnerable parts of the body, which are areas highlighted in the natal chart negated by hard aspects, through guided meditation will also assist the body to guard against cell division; and is perhaps most effective against this type of dis-ease.

If these types of measures are successfully implemented then the body will respond. Likewise, similar to the applied conjunctions, those separating conjunctions will most definitely become a source of healing. Congenital cancer is an indication that little or no suitable measures were implemented in a past life—including the healing powers attached to positive and constructive thought.

These positive and spiritual disciplines will help the soul heal the congenital vibration that weighs heavily. For further information about vitamins and minerals and the guided meditations refer to Chapters 10 and 12.

Chart Data

Grace Brown, October 2, 1931, 13:00 PM in Carshalton UK. Placidus system, mean Node.

Diagnosis, Counterpoint kidney stone decumbiture chart, June 22, 2014, 16:00 PM in Barnstaple UK. Placidus system, mean Node.

Michael Green, July 29, 1948, 3:30 AM in Barnstaple, Devon, UK. Placidus system, mean Node.

Diagnosis, Counterpoint borderline personality disorder decumbiture chart, July 29, 1988, 12:00 PM in Barnstaple Hospital UK. Placidus system, mean Node.

Benjamin Yeo, October 23, 1993, 21:20 PM in Plymouth, Devon, UK. Placidus system, mean Node.

Glen Campbell, April 22, 1936, 20:14 PM in Delight, Arkansas, USA. Placidus system, mean Node.

Diagnosis, Counterpoint Alzheimer's dementia decumbiture chart, January 15, 2011, 12:00 Noon in Phoenix, Arizona, USA. Placidus system, mean node.

Endnotes

[1] My first book, *One Body Many Illnesses*, *An Insightful Approach to Medical Astrology*, was published by the AFA (American Fed-

eration of Astrologers).

[2]In numerology eight is the number represented by Uranus.

[3]According to *Wikipedia* Borderline Personality Disorder also known as Emotionally Unstable Personality Disorder, is a long-term pattern of abnormal behaviour characterized by unstable relationships with other people, unstable sense of self, and unstable emotions. There is often an extreme fear of abandonment, frequent dangerous behaviour, a feeling of emptiness, and self-harm. Symptoms may be brought on by seemingly normal events. The behaviour typically begins by early adulthood, and occurs across a variety of situations. Substance abuse, depression, and eating disorders are commonly associated with BPD. BPD increases the risk of self-harm and 10 percent of people affected die by suicide.

[4]Information source *Wikipedia*.

[5]An excerpt from Kim Campbell's interview with the *Daily Mail* newspaper group.

[6]Dementia occurs at the physical level when a protein called amyloid beta (Neptune) attaches and hardens (Saturn) around the hippocampus in the brain (see Chapter 8, Evolutionary Memory for further information).

Chapter 5

Lunar Causality

"In every man's heart, a spark of fear drives him towards perfection, but in every man's mind, is the inability to endure the heartache of failure."—Benjamin Franklin

Throughout the course of this chapter I would like to examine the cosmic principle known as lunar causality or karma, the unbalanced evolutionary knowledge associated with the Moon and her high points. We begin with the often-unrealized ramifications that are evident and perhaps unavoidable when a distinct lack of spiritual progression from past lives is projected in the current natal chart.

A lack of spiritual progression means that the individual, via his or her free choice, has through the course of evolution turned their back on the divine. The concept of the *divine* characterizes the spiritual substratum representing the seraphic heritage. In most cases, the physical subject possesses little or no recollection of this; however the spiritual body (soul) remains silently aware, and this is often evident via the South Node.

Souls returning to incarnation for the pursuit and gain of Earth plane materialism unfinished business or chemical addiction, places a monumental strain on Earth plane resources. Inevitably, karma is balanced via the Moon and her polarity, Saturn, because the Moon is the custodian and the spiritual healer of the Earth.

Meanwhile, a lack of spiritual progression is shown predominantly in the natal chart as frictional aspects to the Moon, the Black Moon or the South Node; and more so when Venus, Saturn, Neptune and Pluto are indicated. In essence, the individual has opted to return to incarnation in a further attempt to awaken the soul and reclaim his or her spiritual heritage. Frequently, this notion is forgotten once reincarnation into physicality is established.

The esoteric astrologer Nancy B. Detweiler (reference to www.pathwaytoascension.com) touches further upon this formidable truth.

Healing

"Lunar causality characterizes the potential towards the much needed healing of the self."

Lunar causality represents a personalized symbolization of the wisdom of knowledge attained in past lives, which is held within the soul of enlightened individuals. The premise for a "wise soul" is displayed via trines and quintiles to the Sun, the ruler of the Sun, the Moon, and the South Node. Alternatively, this wisdom of knowledge is suppressed and concretized (Saturn the polarity of the Moon) within the soul if there has been little or no spiritual progression; or extreme trauma has occurred throughout previous lives (reference to a life of stasis in Chapter 4). This would suggest the soul was traumatized by an affliction that was consequential in nature and therefore requires healing.

So to reiterate, lunar causality signifies the karma transmitted from our nearest cosmic neighbour: the Moon, and manifests via the North Node (positive) and the South Node; and with the inclusion of the mysterious Black Moon (negative). The Black Moon symbolizes the Moon's apogee (see further on).

A Karmic Lens

Meanwhile, I would like to begin my continued analysis with a deeper inspection of the lunar enigma. The Moon can be likened to a giant magnifying glass that augments and reflects the scintillating energy particles of the Sun. It is within these reflective rays of solar/lunar energy that karma that is directed in the natal chart via the Moon's Nodes.

Equally, it would be a fair hypothesis to suggest that the Moon represents the karmic *lens* of the cosmos—magnifying the knowledge compressed within the essence of lunar causality. The Moon can be likened to a karmic camera reflecting latent images of unresolved past life events projected via the emotional body —transmitted simply as fear or despair, especially through the Black Moon.

This makes the Moon an extremely important and influential component throughout many, if not all, astrological teachings.

A Compendium of Lunar Energy

The Moon is the dispositor of the emotional body. It displays its rulership over the short-term and long-term memory, both of which are vital accessories to our current human perception. I use the term "human perception" because lying deep within the soul, still firmly intact, is the spiritual memory—ruled jointly by the mythical twinned brothers: Neptune and Pluto (reference to Chapter 8: Evolutionary Memory).

Also, the sign that the Moon tenants, which is the essential factor denoting lunar causality, underlines the components of physicality yet to be honed. This means the sign the Moon inhabits most definitely underlines a distinct absence of soul progression.[1]

In addition, the zodiac sign of the South Node can, in the majority of cases, be interpreted in a similar manner to the Moon's sign. This is because the sign the South Node tenants reflects the current level of soul progression, or a lack of it in some cases. If the Moon or the South Node tenants an intercepted house it determines high levels of soul progression. In this case however, the individual concerned needs to draw on all their spiritual awareness in order to remember this forgotten fact.

The Eminences of Lunar Causality

Let us begin with an appropriate example. If the natal Moon, Black Moon or South Node resides in the sign of Taurus the soul most likely languished through a pattern of past life inaction and complacency. With the Moon or her high points in Taurus, the soul's refusal to break free from the shackles that karmically bind it to the mundane routine, coupled by a sheer unwillingness to grab life by the horns is often still evident. A starting point here is further discerned when the Moon and her high points square or oppose planets in fixed signs or succedent houses in the natal chart.

Alternatively, elements that can be positively honed in the current life with the Moon in Taurus are as follows:
- Attaining financial and personal security in the absence of greed and carelessness.
- Embracing and refining creative opportunities in the absence of indecision.
- Not succumbing to indolence and lethargy.
- Acting on instinct.
- A need to acquire sensuality as opposed to obstinacy, obsession and lust.
- Constructing sturdy and robust foundations that have their roots firmly entrenched in solid ground.

In a large percentage of cases where the Moon domiciles resolute Taurus, innate stubbornness and inflexibility are on-going issues that limit the evolutionary progression of the soul. As a result the Moon in Taurus soul adopts a traditional outlook in life. This is because the soul failed to recognize and purge these negative facets throughout the course of its past lives.

Another example of lunar causality, especially when identified as a superior force operating in the natal chart, is when the Moon tenants the restriction-orientated sign of Capricorn. The pervading issue here is to attain heartfelt trust. In the greater percentage of cases souls born with the Moon in Capricorn suppress this life-progressing constituent. Interestingly, Moon in Capricorn souls have actually acquired trust in past lives but their main problem now is that they fail to express it because it is often perceived as fear.

Other facets that are in need of karmically polishing when the Moon tenants Capricorn are:

- Learning to love themselves and others joyously and unconditionally in the absence of fear, sadness and apathy. This is a distinct priority for these souls.
- The individual with this potentially restrictive Moon may have carelessly overlooked his or her inherent abilities in a past life—abilities such as love, compassion and sensitivity.
- These individuals refused to acknowledge or demonstrate these higher emotional characteristics, preferring to keep themselves at a distance. Moon in Capricorn souls have somehow allowed themselves to be emotionally compromised.

It is imperative that the Moon in Capricorn soul learns to trust in him or herself—at which point perhaps he or she will be willing to trust others and their innate sensitivity will come to the forefront. I have seen in so many charts a distinct lack of trines when the Moon tenants Capricorn. It's almost as if Saturn (Capricorn's ruler) has purposely consulted with the Karmic Lords, and between them withdrew these cosmic triangulations for whatever reason—possibly because of unresolved karma. Speaking esoterically, trines represent honed talents from past lives (see further below for more information about this).

If the Moon aspects her Nodal points in the chart (especially via conjunction and opposition) the past life karma is highlighted further. In most cases, when the Moon embraces the Nodes in this way, the lunar influence can often point to several past lives when the soul simply stagnated; thus enduring lifetime after lifetime of drudgery and stasis.

And when examining the Moon for further elements of outstanding karmic law, look at the condition of the Moon sign's planetary ruler to determine the strength and urgency of karma. Look for the type of aspect affecting it. In the previous example of the Moon in Taurus the planetary ruler is of course Venus.

If Venus is void of frictional aspects, or is unaspected, it is quite possible that the current life is implicated in the chart as one of stasis—until; in this case, Venus's lacklustre energy is recognized and altered. This can also be determined by the strength and position of Venus's polarity planet, Mars. Meanwhile, the house position of the Moon and her corresponding aspects to other planets emphasizes potential opportunities to vanquish and conquer these past life occlusions.

Dignities, shown in the case of the Taurus Moon (essential dignity) and the Capricorn Moon (detrimental), and particularly the Moon phase at the time of birth, are also important components to consider when overcoming karma, because they accommodate or impede the soul's potential to move forward on its spiritual path. Also, dignified planets personify the inherent karma. Its position as the closest sphere to the Earth is perhaps one reason why the Moon can be seen as the *modus operandi* of the whole chart—signifying a critical part of astrological law.

Here is a list of the twelve karmic Moon signs:

Lunar Causality via the Moon Signs

- Moon in Aries: unresolved anger and selfishness, an innate need to take control over all aspects of life and others. Frustration and impatience, failure to complete projects and a lack of focus, not taking no for an answer, unrefined and addictive sex drive. Once the lunar karma is purged via the

Nodes (relative to all the Moon signs) the progressed soul with the Moon in Aries strives for the clarity and healing of **Peace**.
- Moon in Taurus (in exaltation): an unwillingness to cooperate, jealousy, stubbornness, fear of moving forward, prone to obsessive and repetitive behaviour, a lack of recognition towards important and life-changing opportunities, a need to manipulate. The progressed soul with the Moon in Taurus exerts towards the power of **Transformation**.
- Moon in Gemini: refusal to acknowledge one's own feelings, academia put before spiritual awareness, duality of the mind, disconnected from reality, shallowness, flightiness and highly-strung, being prone to the "butterfly effect," accident prone. The progressed soul with the Moon in Gemini strives for the gift of **Aspiration**.
- Moon in Cancer (in domicile): festering resentment and grudge-bearing, misunderstanding the fundamental purpose and process of life, paranoia, rigid and inhibited, crabby and stingy, uninspired and lacklustre, mood swings. The progressed soul with the Moon in Cancer strives for the beauty of **Serenity**.
- Moon in Leo: stereotypical attitude, inflexibility, snobby and overbearing, over reacting to minor occurrences, attention seeking, can't teach an old dog new tricks attitude, manipulation of others, eliciting fear in others. The progressed soul with the Moon in Leo exerts towards the humble notion of **Humanitarianism**.
- Moon in Virgo: innate and anxious worrier, a distinct lack of confidence in one's own abilities, a fear of failure, prone to mind disorders such as OCD (Obsessive Compulsive Disorder), hypochondria, fidgety and unsettled, critical of others. The progressed soul with the Moon in Virgo is intuitively guided by the wisdom of **Idealism**.
- Moon in Libra: extreme indecisiveness and unbalanced personality, non-committal, remaining on the fence, refus-

ing to take responsibility for one's actions, prone to mood swings, laziness, unaware and irresponsible. The progressed soul with the Moon in Libra seeks to be embraced with steadfast heroism and **Courage**.

- Moon in Scorpio (in its fall): manipulative and obsessive personality, unforgiving and vengeful, resentful and suspicious, possessive and scheming, enmeshed in unnecessary power struggles, dark and barbarous thoughts. The progressed soul with the Moon in Scorpio strives for wholeness and **Forgiveness**.
- Moon in Sagittarius: the preacher who needs the company of the naive audience, exaggerating, dogmatic and opinionated, Pollyanna, continually pushing their luck, promising too much and failing to honour agreements. The progressed soul with the Moon in Sagittarius is guided by Jovian **Realism**.
- Moon in Capricorn (in detriment): fearful of life situations, avoiding or not recognising life opportunities, not being able to trust oneself and others, prone to depression, unimaginative, authoritarian and cold in expression, stern. The progressed soul with the Moon in Capricorn seeks the power and divinity of heartfelt **Faith**.
- Moon in Aquarius: extreme stubbornness, unbelieving, too independent, believing that it doesn't need anyone else, provocative, explosive personality, erratic and undependable, lack of respect for others, highly-strung, saboteur, disillusioned. The progressed soul with the Moon in Aquarius is bound solely by **Innovation**.
- Moon in Pisces: being a doormat for others to wipe their feet on, lives in a fantasy world often unrealistic personality, in total denial, easily fooled, impractical, deceitful and addictive, easily hurt, prone to escapism. The progressed soul with the Moon in Pisces embraces the heavenliness and wonderment of **Creativity**.

To conclude this chapter I present a scenario involving the popular singer Sir Cliff Richard in order to emphasize the importance of Black Moon in the natal chart.

The Karma of Lunar Causality

According to the Akashic Records the position of the Black Moon in the natal chart determines the point of embarkation to the afterlife. Either the soul will be absorbed into the lower astral (hell) after physical death—depending solely upon the soul's deeds—particularly if a crime of intent is committed without repentance during incarnation.

But equally, the Black Moon represents the point the soul will be absorbed into the higher spirit realms—depending on whether spiritual progression, reflection and healing were the main themes during the soul's incarnation upon the Earth plane.

Sir Cliff Richard and Black Moon Rising

On August 14, 2014, acting on an alleged historical sex allegation, South Yorkshire Police with the assistance of the Thames Valley Police searched a Berkshire property belonging to the singer Sir Cliff Richard. Shockingly, the raid on Sir Cliff's luxury penthouse was televised by the BBC before he had knowledge of any suspected wrongdoing. No arrests were ever made and Sir Cliff, who was in Portugal at the time of the search, said the allegation was "completely false."

Police confirmed later that this single allegation was for a sexual assault that took place at a religious festival in the 1980s involving a boy under the age of 16. Since the original accusation, four more people have also accused Sir Cliff of sexual assault—spanning a period of roughly ten years. On June 16, 2016, after a lengthy police investigation, all the allegations against Sir Cliff were quashed by the Crown Prosecution Service (CPS), due, in part, to insufficient evidence.[3]

So why did these events occur in the first place? To find the

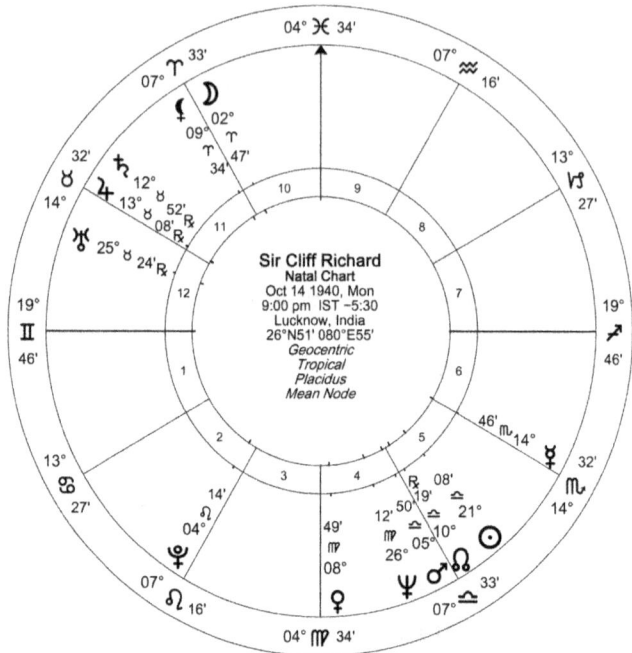

relevant answers we need to examine Sir Cliff Richard's natal chart; and in particular we need to highlight the influence of Black Moon.

Black Moon: A High Point

Black Moon rising is of course a metaphor; it doesn't actually rise on this chart, but it is conjunct the South Lunar Node. The powerful presence of this lunar enigma in Sir Cliff's natal chart, coupled with its unscrupulous influence throughout the police investigation is, in my opinion, wholly responsible for the reverberations attached to this entire unfortunate episode. As for the BBC's coverage of the police raid, this was referred to by the media as a "callous broadcast," that was branded a waste of licence payers' money, and one that resulted in a taint to Cliff Richard's good name indefinitely. Sir Cliff has always maintained his innocence, and to quote his life-long friend the ex British tennis player Sue Barker: "Sir Cliff Richard is a decent and upstanding citizen who has brought pleasure to millions of people throughout his long, illustrious and successful career."

So, what is Black Moon (BM)? Put specifically: If Chiron is a representation of the physical and psychological constraints the soul conveys, or those which have deeply wounded it, then the Black Moon must *accentuate* an emotional impasse.

Repeatedly, I am asked about the potential negative implications it might cast. It is widely believed that Black Moon *accentuates* the darker side of our personality—hidden depths that we truly know exist, yet we prefer not to acknowledge, choosing instead to keep them locked away in the distant recesses and extremities of the subconscious mind. Orthodox teachings indicate that the Black Moon represents an 'index of karma'; hence evil works that purport the sins of man.[2]

Of course this is supposition because from an astropsychological point of view, Black Moon is merely an appearance of the unconscious; a place where human emotion is deemed out of control.

Similar to the Nodes of the Moon, BM represents a point in the heavens rather than an actual planet or stellar body. It should be stressed that Black Moon should not be confused with asteroid 1181 (named Lilith) orbiting in the asteroid belt between Mars and Jupiter. Many astrologers believe it is the apogee of the Moon's orbit. Some believe the perigee represents the White Moon (not to be confused with the actual Moon itself)—though this is rarely acknowledged throughout many western astrological teachings.[3]

Dark Matter

Metaphorically, Black Moon represents a void of empty dark matter in space—except that space is anything but empty. Hence, BM is an area of *empty focus*, the second focal point of the elliptical orbit of the Moon around the Earth, where every aspect of hidden emotional turmoil such as guilt, envy, jealousy, shame, hatred vengefulness and even cold-heartedness congregate, creating an eclipsing soup of negativity.

There are only a handful of astrologers who include this critical point in their chart analysis, but I have always found the Black Moon to be associated with the impending levels of emotional karma the soul brings forth into incarnation. One such example is shown in the natal chart of the North Korean dictator Kim Jong-un who has the Black Moon conjunct his natal Moon in the sign of Pisces. This would signify that he carries within his psyche a great deal of desolation, anger and guilt. These emotional traits are often displayed via his often naive demeanour. At the physical level he has not yet acquired the benefit of emotional stability, and it is clear he was openly rejected by his mother. It also seems clear that emotional instability has caused his soul to fragment in some way.[4] In effect, the influence of the Black Moon in his chart is as influential as if he had incarnated with the Sun and the Moon square to each other.

In a horoscope, the BM is the point in which we experience the greatest challenge. In effect, BM is our blind spot. Therefore, BM must first be extricated and purged then drawn upon as a source of great strength, positivity and resourcefulness. Once we have overcome the obstacles posed by BM, the essence of this lunar point can be brought into the light and successfully healed. Only then will we be able to see clearly beyond the confines posed by this lunar blind spot.

Black Moon is a moving mass of lunar energy slowly advancing through the zodiac in a nine-year cycle, and can be a major influence in chart interpretation. Nevertheless, I don't believe that this important lunar enigma should be viewed in the same way as the planets and their cycles. The influences of the transiting natal planets to Black Moon are the best constituents to use when interpreting its karmic influence in the chart. Although, it works just as powerfully when it makes transits to natal planets.

The Black Moon Natal Chart: A Karmic Hub

Significantly, Black Moon resides at nine degrees of Aries (true BM[5] in Sir Cliff Richard's natal chart (Aries signifying injustice). BM resides in the eleventh house, and tightly conjoins the Nodes, and is also in a wide conjunction to the Moon from the tenth (using Placidus houses). Speaking generally, the modern ruler of the eleventh house (denoting ostracism) is of course Uranus, and Uranus resides in the adjoining twelfth house of karma in Taurus (detrimental). We can speculate here that Sir Cliff was held captive against his free will at some point throughout his evolution. The ancient ruler of the eleventh house and modern ruler of the tenth is Saturn, and Saturn also resides in the eleventh in a tight conjunction with Jupiter—making the eleventh house the focal point of karma for the entire chart. This, in my opinion, gives more nuance to the being held captive theory.

In addition, the planetary rulership of Black Moon (Mars) tenants Libra (detrimental) and opposes this lunar enigma, and with Pluto residing in the second/third—the second being its natural polarity house.[6] If we were to assume the Ascendant is influenced by Mars and the Black Moon, then it could easily denote suppressed anger and rage. Also, the Sun tenants the fifth house also in detriment (in its fall in Libra). Venus is of course the ruler of Libra (Libra signifying justice) and communicates incomprehensibly to Black Moon via the adjustment-orientated quincunx from the sign of Virgo (detrimental). This indicates that an adjustment needs to be achieved somehow, whereby the scales must be rebalanced via the attainment of credible justice. Venus also rules Taurus where it casts its hallowed shadow over Uranus. Neptune tenants the angular fourth house in Virgo—also in detriment.

A further connection in this spider's web of mystery and intrigue is the Moon also residing in Aries (traditionally Aries ruling the first house). The Moon's sign of Cancer is, in this example, the accidental ruler of the first house sharing this personal domain with Mercury-ruled Gemini, with Mercury residing at the cusp of the fifth/sixth houses—Mercury traditionally ruling the sixth. Healing the emotional and psychological centres of the physical body is imperative.

The karmic pieces of this Black Moon-orientated natal chart slot together like some outlandish jigsaw puzzle, but with a hint of past life redemption. With so many planets in dignity (five in total), and three retrograde planets, coupled with Black Moon perched at the top of the chart (elevated), the objectives in this chart are that each of the interplanetary influences must be brought into consciousness for the purposes of soul healing preferably through attaining justice for his soul.

I would describe Black Moon in Aries as essentially a potent combination of exasperation and highly-emotional charged particles of energy.

Property Search

In this event chart (the police raid on Sir Cliff Richard's home) the concerning factors are Pluto (ruler of Scorpio) and its square to Cliff Richard's natal Black Moon; and Mars (dignified) with its separating quincunx to Cliff Richard's BM. Interestingly, both Mars and Saturn (the malefic planets conjoining) and the Ascendant tenant Scorpio, the sign that rules the police. Also, the waning Moon makes a conjunction to Cliff Richard's natal Black Moon. Neptune dignified in Pisces tenants the fourth house, representing the home, in an exact quincunx to Jupiter. Mercury at 27 Leo, an Azimene (deficient) degree, applies its influence to Neptune in a wide opposition. Leo and Pisces are disassociating signs suggesting again the quincunx factor.

With so much frictional activity this chart highlights a definite cause for concern over the plight of the popular singer. However, the transiting North Node tenants Libra from the twelfth house of karma and the North Node forms a sextile to the Sun and the Sun trines Uranus, which conjoins the South Node (Uranus

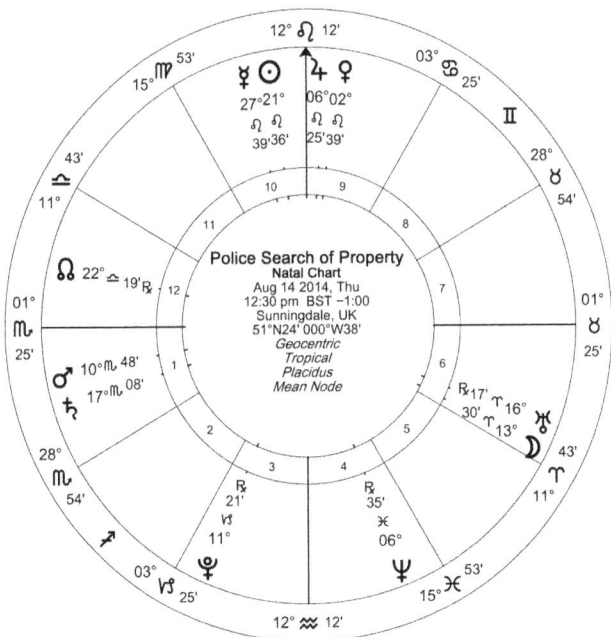

being one of the factoring planets in Sir Cliff's natal chart with its general rulership of the eleventh house, the focal point of his chart's karma, as already discussed), indicating that justice may well prevail here for him. Neptune's trine to the Ascendant and Mars, and Venus and Jupiter's (the benefics) conjunction to the Black Moon probably saves the day. Interestingly, no arrest was ever made as a result of this unprecedented incursion.

Acquittal

Perhaps the most significant finding in this event (acquittal) chart is that Libra (sign of justice) sits on the cusp of the eleventh house at 9 degrees using Placidus houses (a Pluto degree in numerology). This is the same degree as Sir Cliff's natal Black Moon (true BM) in his eleventh house, though in the opposite sign. Also, in this chart, and depending on the software used, the mean Black Moon at 15 Scorpio (the police) appears in the

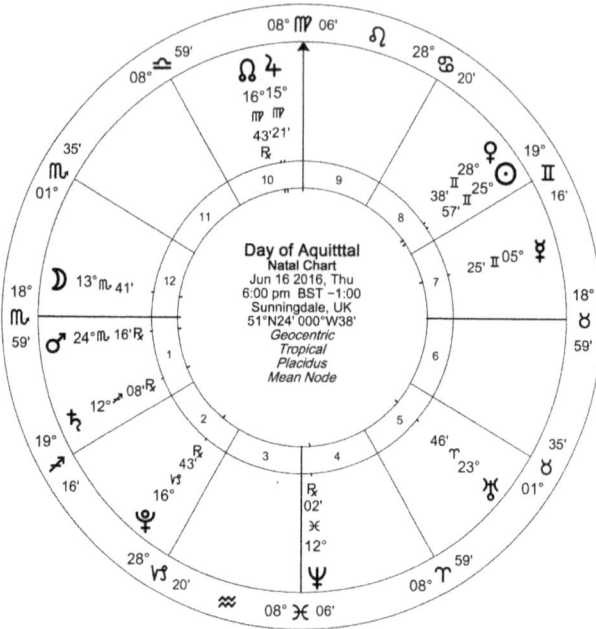

twelfth house of retribution. Retrograde Saturn (karma) applies via a trine to Cliff Richard's natal Black Moon, and Neptune is once again residing in the fourth house closely conjoined the South Node. Jupiter (lord luck) conjoins the North Node.

The question must surely be, has justice finally been done and will further justice prevail? These are powerful cosmic significators that indicate a triumphant conclusion. Really, can Sir Cliff finally put this torrid affair behind him? Well with the finger of God (Yod) pointing to a retrograde and dignified Mars on the Ascendant from the Sun and Uranus in sextile formation at the Yod's base, I would say there is every chance that he will be completely exonerated, and his good name restored.

I do, however, envisage repercussions on the South Yorkshire Police Force, as a result of their cavalier attitude (Venus quincunx to Mars)—possibly beginning with a complex review examining their outdated procedures—and sudden closure (Uranus quincunx to Mars) of this particular force. Whether or not Sir Cliff's legal challenge in the high court brings closure to the karmic cycle is another matter, but with Venus and Uranus in sextile formation I suspect it may very well do.

But, despite the eventual outcome, I feel conclusively that it will help to heal his soul. So, watch this space folks!

Conclusion

In my opinion, Sir Cliff Richard is wholly innocent of the allegations that he stands accused of. The position of Black Moon in his natal chart (in Aries at 9 degrees true BM, and a Pluto degree, and in the karmically-charged eleventh house), coupled with retrograde Uranus in the twelfth house, advocates that his accusers are most probably the guilty party here in this complex and karmic scenario (vengeful perpetrators from an unfortunate past life).

Thus, it is a fair assumption to convene that his accusers are guilty of reigniting the karmic flames of injustice—burning in his soul throughout countless incarnations—stoked in this life by the Nodal polarity in his natal chart. Recently, it has come to the forefront that his accusers are all in fact convicted criminals, one of which was blackmailing him (Neptune). Another was a convicted paedophile (paedophilia could in fact be connected to BM in Aries).

A further metaphorical implication, and one that is exacerbated by Uranus's occupation of the twelfth house and Neptune's detrimental occupation of the fourth house (traditionally ruled by the Moon), is that in a previous life his accusers were his despot jailers. His home (fourth house) was within the confines of a dirty (Neptune) and cramped prison cell (Saturn's contraction effect over Jupiter)— incarcerated for crimes he didn't commit (Neptune detrimental in Virgo and Mercury in Scorpio opposing Saturn and Jupiter all denoting misunderstandings).

With so many planets in detriment and significant linkages

between all three charts this particular karmic cycle of injustice will no doubt be difficult to bring into consciousness (the light) for the purpose of healing. But with Mars in its polarity sign of peace-loving Libra and opposing Black Moon, and Venus the ruler of Libra tenanting the fourth house, this chain of events may actually be the catalyst for the healing process to begin. Only time will tell!

As previously indicated, Sir Cliff Richard has strongly indicated that he will sue South Yorkshire Police and the BBC for the unauthorised and televised raid on his property. Perhaps this is what's required in order to rebalance the Libra archetypal scales that have been seriously damaged.

However, if Black Moon is also a representation of the Moon's feminine quality,[7] we can surmise that in the unconscious and to coin one of Sir Cliff Richard's songs, Black Moon really is the *Devil Women* in disguise in his natal chart. But, in retrospect, I like to think that Sir Cliff's long-term commitment to the world of popular music (especially the many ballads he has sung over the years) is what has helped and continues to heal and thus rebalance his soul (Neptune and Venus—the higher and lower octave vibration). May he continue to find eternal peace!

Chart Data

Sir Cliff Richard, October 14, 1940, 21:00 PM in Lucknow, India. Placidus houses, mean Node.

Police Search of Property, August 14, 2014, 12:30 PM in Sunningdale, Berkshire, UK. Placidus houses, mean Node.

Day of Acquittal, June 16, 2016, 18:00 at CPS Headquarters, London, UK. Placidus houses, mean Node.

Endnotes

[1] Information source *Wikipedia*.
[2] From Biblical Astrology.
[3] This point, the Moon's perigee, is called *Priapus* by French as-

trologers. 'White Moon' might be a confusing term because the actual Moon itself is often called the White Moon (the White Goddess). Information source Paul F. Newman.

[4] Information source *Astrotheme*.

[5] Mean and True Apogees of BM. The Mean and True positions of BM are based on two estimations of the Moon's current orbit similar to the Nodes. Neither can be said to be right or wrong, because at the moment you request the position of the Moon's apogee, the Moon is simply where it is, and projecting where it would be if it was at apogee is hypothesised whatever formula is used—Astro Dienst. Basically, "mean" means average and 'true' means exact.

[6] According to the Russian astrologer Albert R. Timashev "planets that frequent their polarity house are similar to fish out of water."

[7] Carl Jung, the famous psychoanalyst, described something that he referred to as the "anima." According to Jung "the anima is a man's image of the ideal women and also the feminine side of his personality. For women the 'animus' is the image of the ideal man and the masculine side of her personality." So Black Moon in the natal chart also represents these ideals.

Chapter Six

Healing via the Application of Color

"The pain of the mind is worse than the pain of the body."—Publilius Syrus, Roman Writer and Poet, 1st Century BC

The concept of healing via the application of color begins solely with the current human condition; but more precisely it begins with the expulsion of the corrupted and heavy vibrations surrounding the human condition. Allow me to explain!

Presently, the interconnected vibrations of color present on the Earth plane, especially those in the natural world, resonate at a much lower vibration than they did millennia ago. This is why solid matter appears to be featureless and in a state of temporary flux. However, this overall appearance is generally accepted as being the norm. Regrettably, color is no longer defined, and doesn't sparkle as colors continue to do on the elevated spirit levels. Responsible for the onset of these lower vibrations of color is pollution and a lack of collective awareness, caused in part by the human inclination towards persistent reincarnation that is often *static* by definition.

Being continually dragged back by the dominant pull of Earth plane physicality, we prefer physical embodiment as opposed to progressing onwards through the spirit levels. Unfortunately, for a multitude of souls, the Earth has become a static base where the illusion of misconception can be reproduced time and time again. If this flawed notion isn't altered the Earth will once again begin the process of cataclysm, starting around the year 2068 when Pluto (representing the violet vibration) completes its current passage through the zodiac.

The mass of individuals who merely exist via a life of stasis is at an all-time high.[1] Spiritual progression on the Earth plane or in the spirit world should ideally raise the soul's vibration, including the clarity and density of the aura. Thus, higher vibrations of color density are necessary for soul healing.

Throughout the course of millennia the colors of the soul projected through the aura have become tarnished because of the pull and the illusion of the Earth in its disconnected, polluted and twisted state of confinement. Today, the aura (the spiritual reflection of the soul energy) is the singular vibration that protects the physical body, screening it from potential harm. Unfortunately, the decreases in the vibrational color resonances of the aura caused by the contamination of the Earth plane, are responsible for the onset of illness and disease.

Long ago, the Earth, coruscating in all its splendour and glory, formed a backdrop to a perfectly aligned and interconnected cosmos comprising scores of colored energy patterns. Every pattern was further enhanced by a shimmering combination of translucent color. For the most part, many souls have become blind and disassociated from this spiritual reality, preferring to view only the mirage associated with man-made materialism.

It was via this array of planetary color that the soul originally discovered its progressive purpose, quest for knowledge and desire to return to the Godhead.

Impassive Planetary Vibrations

Every planet throughout the cosmos resonates at a specific wave length vibration, projecting a dynamic confluence of color.

These colored planetary vibrations are loosely integrated and projected via the human aura. I use the term "loosely" because until the physical karma has been balanced the colors of the aura continue to remain characterless and imbalanced.

Although the aura can be likened to a protective blanket of integrated colored energy, at certain periods throughout life this blanket becomes kinked due to the stresses of frictional planetary alignments. These frictional planetary alignments symbolize the karmic processes at work that balance the aura, and therefore balance the soul's karma.

Often, and as a result of hard aspects, the aural colors become hazy and muddied as the transiting planet/planets assert their powerful and life-altering influences. Once the planet/planets have completed the necessary life-altering work and completed their karmic mission, the color/colors symbolized by the transiting planet/planets purge and transcend the aura—instrumental in spiritual revitalisation. At least that is the theory!

Once this transcension of altered color has been achieved the aura becomes much more defined; meaning the vibrational energy of precise planetary color is now firmly integrated into the chakral energy field. At the culmination point of the physical journey (death) the aura should ideally be a shimmering and pristine energy field complete with multiple coloured energy patterns symbolizing the honed and integrated planetary energies.

The soul is then transformed into the beautifully-polished and faceted jewel it was originally before it began again its journey in the murky and contaminated pool of physicality—ready to begin its transition once more through the spirit world.[2]

The Color Spectrum of Planetary Aspects

Before I begin, it is important to reiterate that the fallen souls who commit acts of unadulterated depravity and terror choose to do so because they are simply void of any internal consciousness.

This absence of consciousness has occurred because, technically speaking, they have manifested through evolution as individuals who are indeed soulless. In other words, there is an absence of any sharp and defined color contained within the aura, creating an imbalance within the soul's fragmented energy field.

Those fallen souls need to transmute the vibrancy of their heart centre to a higher resonant frequency in order to balance the aura and draw in additional color. Outlining such a transition will allow them to take measures towards the first step to reconnect themselves to their very essence (the soul). In this way they can distinguish elemental truths such as the difference between right and wrong. Raising Neptune's vibration to the soul level will help to achieve this.

Souls who refuse to traverse a conscious path towards the supernal light remain permanently in a monotonous gray mode. A dull or featureless gray is often regarded by color therapists as an inferior and substandard color vibration of low intensity. However, if the gray vibration is viewed as vibrant within the aura, for example coruscating as silver, it is then revered as an energizing, revitalizing and nurturing vibration of color.

When planets align to form aspects (gravitational fields of energy) luminescent vibrations of color are created between the planets that can be visualized via meditation. Aspects occur between planets for the purpose of healing and zodiacal degrees indicate the level and intensity of the healing required. So, for example, a sextile (60 degrees = 6) is a Venus ruled aspect (see planetary list of numbers), and sextiles are ideal aspects to enable the soul to overcome trauma, physically or mentally. The color that forms between the connecting planets of the sextile (not the colors of the planets themselves that are listed in the final chapter) is a rich and luminescent emerald green; an excellent aspect for healing the heart chakra. Whether they are natal or transiting sextiles, these endearing aspects help us to embrace the opportunities posed by the frictional aspects.

A natal trine (120 degrees = 3) is a Jupiter ruled aspect possessing energy similar to the sextile, although it is multiplied. The colour is a deep, intense, almost translucent violet. Sextiles and trines are considered to be benefic aspects. Natal trines represent talents honed in past lives (more about this in the chapter Developing Dis-eases). Semi-sextiles (30 degrees = 3) are also Jupiter ruled configurations, but the colour that forms between this foundation-building and directional aspect is a pale pink. Though considered to be minor, by their very nature semi-sextiles are warm and cathartic aspects, depending on how they are perceived. Human perception, in most cases, determines the very nature of this inconjunct aspect.

Transiting trines have a similar effect to sextiles; the color that forms between them is a metallic hue reminiscent of royal blue. Quincunxes (150 degrees = 6) are slightly different in vibrational density and astrological configuration. These aspects are essentially karmic, and thus difficult to master. Quincunxes are ruled jointly by Venus and Pluto. Their colors, or translucent shades, are a crystalline form of black until their effects are transcended, then their energies transmute into pure white light—vibrational resonances manifesting similar to that of the conjunction.

Frictional aspects in the natal chart, either natal or transiting, such as semi-squares (45 degrees = 9), squares (90 degrees = 9), sesquisquadrates (135 degrees = 9) and oppositions (180 degrees = 9) are all Pluto ruled. The colors that form between these right angles and polarized aspects are black and crimson red (the square aspects), and purple lake and magenta (the opposition).

Frictional aspects such as squares and oppositions provide a lifetime of challenges and duality and therefore require a lifetime of intense diplomacy and the positive healing of challenge if their rewards are to be successful. Frictional aspects are transmuted into trines in future incarnations, providing of course they have been suitably mastered, balanced and learned from.[3]

Using an aural imaging camera the strength of the individual colors and the arc with which the colors extend within the aura can be viewed with relative ease. Prominent colors within the aura generally symbolize the colors of the planets that are a part of the honed aspect/aspects in the natal chart.

If the soul has experienced countless incarnations of honing frictional aspects in order to acquire higher-mindedness (wisdom) then aspects highlighting extraordinary skills are displayed in the natal chart, indicating exceptional levels of soul growth and progression. Higher-minded aspects include: vigintiles (18 degrees—gold and Pluto), deciles (36 degrees – gold and Pluto), septiles (51 degrees, silver and blue and Venus), quintiles and bi-quintiles (72 and 144 degrees respectively, golden yellow and Pluto). All these aspects possess the capability to link the heart-mind directly to the Godhead.

Conjunctions (zero degrees) are neutral aspects and the color that emerges before the planets reach the orb of zero is brilliant white. Conjunctions are celestial healing aspects that open up cosmic doorways into unknown possibilities. A list of aspectual colorations is displayed in detail throughout Chapter 12: Guided Meditations.

All these higher-mind aspects assist the soul with its healing process because they share a rulership under Venus, Neptune and Pluto —healing from the constant trauma relayed by frictional aspects (see Chapter 7, Predominant Healing Aspects, for further information).

Planetary Patterns

Finishing with some important points here would be to highlight that individual aspectual colorations still apply in the same way where multiple planetary configurations are concerned, such as Grand Crosses, Grand Trines and Yods etc. So, for example, the Grand Trine would pulsate in a rich and vibrant royal blue similar to the trine.

Also, the individual degree of each zodiac sign emits a unique vibrational color. These geometrically derived colors will be listed in a future publication.

Planetary Retrogrades

If there are retrograde planets in an aspect alignment, the colors will alter. This is due, in part, to a juxtapositional shift in the planet's influence. The optical illusion known as retrograde or backward motion evokes even more intricate and whimsical shades of color. A complete list of the aspectual colors for retrograde motions can also be found in the final chapter: Guided Meditations.

Numerical Vibrations of the Planets

- The Sun: zero
- Mars: one
- The Moon: two
- Jupiter: three
- Saturn: four
- Mercury: five
- Venus: six
- Neptune: seven
- Uranus: eight
- Pluto: nine

The Duration of Illness and Disease

When one or more planetary patterns have been indentified in the natal or decumbiture chart as likely catalysts for the onset of an illness or disease, the duration of the illness can also be ascertained by multiplying the planetary numbers.

So, for example, if we examine the kite type formation involving Venus in Pisces (Venus being six in numerology and dignified in Pisces) and Saturn in Sagittarius (Saturn being four and retrograde) forming a square, and Mars (Mars being number one and denoting pain) forming a quincunx to Saturn (the hardening effect) and a sextile to Venus (completing the kite), the duration of the ensuing illness will be equal to the addition of these numbers, so approximately eleven days in length. However, if the illness or disease persists or it is diagnosed as terminal then the duration may be extended to eleven months or even years. In either case the number eleven will always configure in the astrological equation.

Following on with the example of eleven days, the particular dis-ease that was diagnosed was sciatica; and sciatica can be mainly attributed to Sagittarius, which has its rulership over the sciatic nerve. The severity of the sciatica would be governed by the malefic planets (Mars and Saturn) that were involved in this particular pattern.

I established this formula recently in April 2017. Here a client was diagnosed with sciatica as a result of the aforementioned kite formation in his natal chart involving Venus, Mars and Saturn. The pattern was located in the intercepted zones of his chart giving it an additional distinction and strength. Shortly after, the condition worsened when Mars made a hard quincunx to Saturn from Taurus completing the kite pattern (Taurus being his opposite sign in this case). In my opinion, quincunx aspects become exceptionally powerful when they connect to major aspects, especially from a medical viewpoint.

The symptoms of sciatica began to subside, allowing the healing process to begin after eleven days had elapsed. I have used this formula with other clients, and each of their illnesses began to subside within the number of days governed by the planetary aspects involved. Light therapy using the colors represented by those planets also helped to alleviate the symptoms (see Chapter 12, Guided Meditations).

The Planets and Death (Departing the Physical Body)

Similar to the birth (life) path number that exemplifies a particular planetary influence in numerology denoting prestigiousness, the death path number on the day you vacate your physical body determines influences present on the journey ahead, through the higher spirit realms, purgatory or the lower astral. So, for example, if you pass on a numerological four day (Saturn) or a nine day (Pluto), the journey ahead will be a time of reconciliation. In most cases, passing on a six day (Venus) will determine that a time of peace and harmony lies ahead.

More about this in my forthcoming publication: *Astrology for Self-Mastery.*

Endnotes

[1] Evolutionary statistics retrieved from the Akashic Records.

[2] Modified information by which the original transcripts are contained within the Akashic Records.

[3] Astrological law and colourations is a concept that is equally endorsed by the esoteric astrologer and psychic Nancy B. Detweiler.

Chapter 7

Predominant Healing Aspects

"Astrology is the blueprint of the forces that flow into the body and maintain it."—Dr William M. Davidson

Planetary dialogues, or aspects, as they are more commonly referenced, are perhaps the foundation blocks of astrology. The Australian astrologer Christine Broadbent, eloquently referred to the planetary aspects as the "dances of the cosmos" in a time-honoured article.[1] This notion determines that the planets and their aspects are finely woven into the divine tapestry of the Godhead—intertwined with exceptional quality thread to which its microcosmic fibres resonate as a perfectly-aligned blend of psychoanalytical and spiritual energy.

A few of these interplanetary alignments represent spiritual sounding boards; meaning that their energies are projected at a higher frequency of vibration. It may be crucial to refer to these as: "predominant healing aspects." This is not to say that other planetary aspects are not important or influential, each is expressed through its own unique resonance field of vibration.

I hope to expand further on the concept of what I refer to as Predominant Healing Aspects via some well known celebrity case studies.

Followng are celebrity case studies.

The Conjunction: Unification

According to astrologer Alan Oken,[2] "a conjunction (comprising three or more planets) signifies a burst of energy that emanates from combined cosmic diversities and distant dimensional sources." Also, and according to the astrologer Alice A. Bailey, "our gifts are tokens bearing remembrance from the unified divine."[3]

The conjunction is the powerful aspect that culminates at *nil* or zero degrees—with an orb either side of eight degrees. The purpose of the conjunction is *unification*, hence a complete emergence of psychological, physical and spiritual energies for the purpose of consolidation. Conjunctions coin the phrase: "two heads are better than one." Obviously, when there are more than two planets forming the conjunction the potential highlighted by the configuration is multiplied further.

Conjunctions (mostly comprising two planets) signify hierarchal energies are at work. So, for example, someone who has the Sun conjunct Mercury in the natal chart would possess a powerful brain capable of thinking outside of the box so to speak, especially if—say—Uranus also configured in the equation by trine. If however, the Sun and Mercury were aspected to Neptune via a hard aspect, the person would possess a powerful brain but with also a tendency not to use it.

So, we can use an example of someone who has the Sun conjunct Mercury again, but this time *conjoined* to Uranus as opposed to being trined by it. Here the individual would not only be capable of thinking outside of the box, but their thought patterns would be radical in nature, coupled with humanistic idealism. Once the conjunction is honed they may even be interested in scientific paradigms and multidimensional concepts such as quantum mechanics.

In my opinion conjunctions are cosmic significators—highlighting that we emanate from a unified group soul in the spirit world—particularly when Neptune configures.

Keywords for the Conjunction:
- Difficult attributes—tension, evasion, separation, refusal to acknowledge life situations, visionless and unsighted, claustrophobic, destructive, loss of perspective.
- Constructive attributes—harmony via oneness, united in perspective, distinguishing between the senses, blending of the senses, superior intellect, spiritual balance, acceptance, problem solving.

Adele

In the natal chart of the British popular singer Adele, there are two prominent and influential conjunctions. Notably, they are "predominant healing aspects." The first is an exact conjunction between Venus and Chiron at their Counterpoint (see natal chart). Both planets tenant the sign of Gemini (cerebral). The Moon opposes the conjunction from the sign of Sagittarius (directional).

The second conjunction involves the Sun and Jupiter gracing its influence from the sign of Taurus (consolidating). Dignified Pluto from Scorpio (transformational) opposes it; and Mars provides additional weight to the conjunction by the way of a dynamic square. Although there are no major aspects between the two conjunctions Venus nevertheless connects them, being the domicile ruler of Taurus. Therefore, the Sun/Jupiter conjunction can be deemed a 'pre-directional' configuration, meaning that Adele will always and instinctively discover direction that she is meant to pursue at every step of her journey. This conjunction is extremely auspicious because it represents a harbinger for luck and fortune—shadowed by sheer weight of evolutionary transformation.

Recently, it was reported that Adele is prone to suffering from severe bouts of depression and anxiety disorder.[4] The square from Mars to the Sun and to Jupiter, coupled with Pluto's opposition are likely to be the culprits for these dark-centred indispositions.

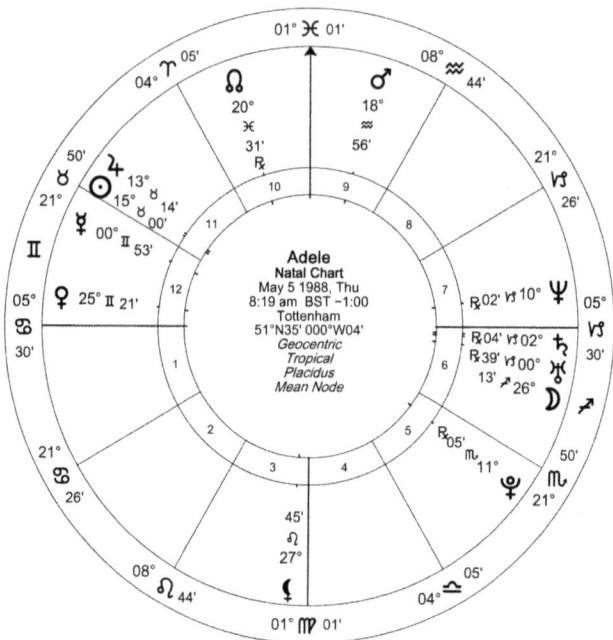

However, Venus and Chiron's Counterpoint has the potential to help her overcome depression because Chiron provides healing. Healing will be particularly relevant when transit Jupiter conjoins natal Pluto in Scorpio in the latter part of 2017, forming a transformational conjunction. Also, the Jupiter in Scorpio opposition to itself and her natal Sun is likely to instil a wholly new set of circumstances, allowing her to alter direction from the steadfast confines of her singing career—particularly when transit Jupiter reaches the midpoint of the Sun/Jupiter conjunction in 2017. New direction is also likely to be confirmed once Jupiter domiciles Sagittarius in 2018.

In my opinion, Adele will begin traversing new ground from the latter half of 2018. Thanks to the healing potential of the Venus-Chiron conjunction, triggered by transit Jupiter's trine to it earlier in 2017. Meanwhile, she can now begin overcoming her depression and anxiety by embracing new direction (Jupiter) and orchestrating new creative ventures (the Sun). Rather than "chasing pavements," to coin her 2007 first hit single, she can look forward to quality healing by chasing and securing new directions, courtesy of the all-powerful Venus-Chiron Counterpoint, coupled with complete physical and spiritual unification.

In addition, her life will begin to feel fully healed if she chooses to acknowledge and embrace the gift of service that she offers to disadvantaged children, as highlighted by Saturn and Uranus's conjunction with the inclusion of Neptune opposing her Cancer Ascendant.

The Sextile: Expedience

The sextile is a 60-degree neutral aspect that requires *activation*. Let me explain. Most aspects are experienced naturally either in a physical or in a psychological capacity, without any additional understanding required. They are simply perceived as positive or negative influences felt within the physical mainframe of the body. Sextiles bring a sense of completion and clarity to the semi-sextile and the quincunx (inconjunct aspects that are often a source of confusion).

Aspects that require *activation* like the sextile are somewhat different, because only via the process of heartfelt meditation and spiritual awareness can they be employed to their fullest potential. I have heard some astrologers refer to sextiles as aspects of "little or no significance." Once again, this is because they need to be activated at the soul level of consciousness. Then an opportunity for advancement and healing will present itself. Meditation, particularly breath meditation, automatically activates the sextiles, as they mysteriously become attached to the soul as a means of harnessing awareness and enhancing progression.

Keywords for the Sextile:
- Difficult attributes—missed opportunities, secretive, lack of direction, flawed idealism, uncooperative, stagnation, materialistic, unbalanced.

- Constructive attributes—opportunistic, divine assistance, reinforcement of natural creativity, openness, positive growth, idealism, cooperation, opening spiritual portals.

Tom Hanks

In the natal chart of the distinguished American actor Tom Hanks there are two influential and opportunistic sextiles (see natal chart). Once again, they are both "predominant healing aspects."

The first is a sextile between Jupiter and Neptune. This is a disassociated aspect because Jupiter is at zero degrees of Virgo (the organizer), and its influence is weakened slightly because the planet of luck and fortune is at its fall in Virgo. In this case, and for the conventional sextile to form, it would require Jupiter to tenant Leo at 27 degrees and Neptune at 27 degrees of Libra respectively. Both these sextiled planets represent the natural polarity of Mercury (Jupiter and Neptune being rulers of Pisces), and this gives additional nuance to the opportunity offered by the sextile aspect.

The second sextile involves Neptune and Pluto in a separating Counterpoint. In both cases Saturn squares Jupiter and Pluto and acts as the initializer to both the sextiles.

Hanks has type 2 diabetes. The catalyst for this all too common affliction is likely to be Mars (insulin) from the sixth house of health opposing Hanks's Ascendant in Virgo (the sign ruler of the pancreas). Pluto is also deemed in modern astrology the planetary ruler of the pancreas.

All the signs in the natal chart point to the diabetes being a karmic affliction. The obvious pointer has to be Mercury's quincunx to the Moon's North Node and its semi-sextile to the South Node —connecting Mercury's agile and quick thinking influence to the sextiles. This configuration implies that diabetes has been a factor in previous lives but needs to be moderated and contained within the current life. Mercury's quincunx to the

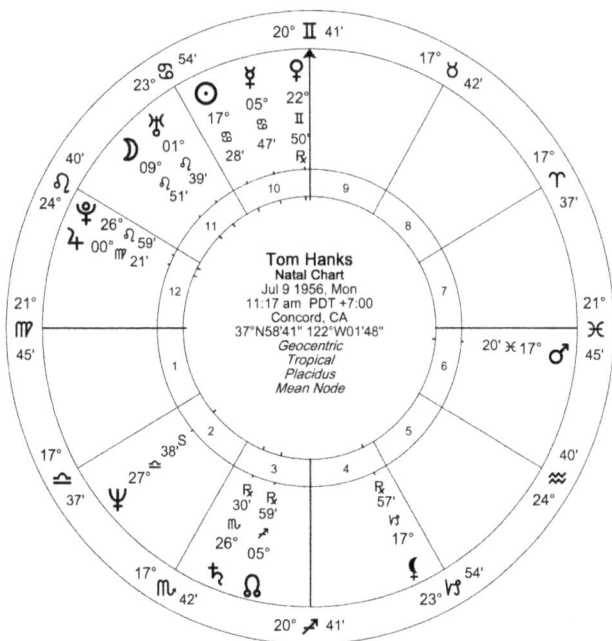

North Node in Sagittarius highlights the karmic effect, symbolizing further Jupiter's position from the twelfth house of karma and past lives.

Diabetes occurs when life's sweetness is blotted out. The Neptune-Pluto sextile at its Counterpoint ought to provide Hanks with the opportunity to heal his soul from this karmic affliction by relighting the internal flame of hope, whereby he could discover his inner creator and in turn save himself from the outer turmoil caused by the family problems[5] that have beset his life. These personal family difficulties are conveyed partly by the Sun's opposition to the Black Moon in the fourth house.

In addition, the Neptune-Pluto sextile is an advantageous aspect, implying immense expediency towards soul healing. Saving himself and others from the advent of potential catastrophe is what Hanks does best—remarkably portrayed in the films: *Sully*, *Saving Private Ryan* and *Cast Away*.

The Square: Stimulus

The square is a 90-degree aspect whose energy is often considered *undefined*, meaning that the square makes its presence felt in a challenging but rather unfamiliar way — as if tucked away within the undefined recesses of the periphery vision. Let me explain. For healing to take place the square must be transformed into a tool that rebalances the spirit/soul. The challenges posed by the square must be honed at the soul level of consciousness.

Metaphorically speaking, squares are aspects that form a part of our periphery vision. Usually however, our periphery vision is not fully defined, and that is what the energy of a square is — some invisible powerful force that is undefined. Squares only manifest as positive influences if what is instinctively defined on the periphery vision turns out to be favourable; in other words if the perceived entity is friendly. On the other hand if the entity is perceived as unfriendly then the square often becomes a cause for concern—a major challenge, even a stumbling block on the life path.

Keywords for the Square:
- Difficult attributes—conflict of interest, hardships, complications, power struggles, inability for self-expression, fear, obstacles, extreme stress.
- Constructive attributes—stimulation of the senses, persistence, heartfelt success, enhancing the energy of the soul, progressive growth, overcoming obstacles, positive creativity, and peripheral *agent provocateur*.

Keanu Reeves

Keanu Reeves is perhaps best known for his movie portrayal as Neo in the film *The Matrix*. Neo is a futuristic character—projecting an ambience that is dark and tenebrous. The whole concept of the Neo characterization is reminiscent of the square; hence a predominant healing aspect. Furthermore, Reeves has more recently been considered by his peers as a profound and creative "visionary."

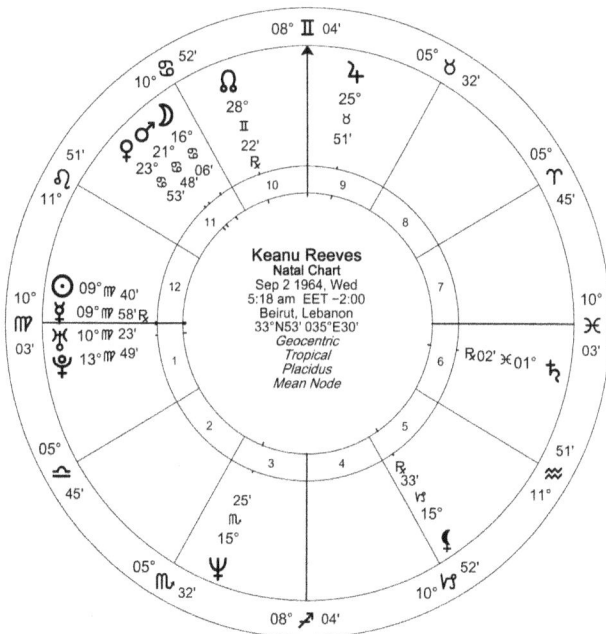

This notion is certainly applicable given the position of Uranus in his natal chart at its Counterpoint to the Ascendant—just in the first house and squared to the Midheaven (see natal chart). Technically speaking, Uranus is besieged between Mercury and Pluto, and presided over by an empirical Ascendant. This could suffocate Uranus, the planet of higher ideals, and create a radical need to liberate the inner spirit via self-analysis, for it is his inner spirit that is in need of healing. Reeves is propelled towards attaining perfection according to his acting colleagues. This assumption gives rise to certain elements that dominate the personal sector of his chart, prevailed upon by angular Pluto sitting close to his Virgo Ascendant.

Keanu Reeves is dyslexic, and perfectionism is an idiosyncrasy often associated with dyslexia.[6] In the natal chart, dyslexia can be attributed to the exact conjunction of the Sun and Mercury. (Mercury being dignified) in a separating Counterpoint, which is also conjunct Uranus—squared to the MC. Neptune is connected to this configuration via a sextile to Pluto, Uranus and the Ascendant. Neptune tenants the third house; the medical zone often associated with dyslexia. The Virgo stellium is at the midpoint of the trine between the Moon and Neptune. Also, the Neptune influence gives nuance to the theory that Reeves has been referred to as a visionary.

It does seems clear that Reeves had instinctively accepted the challenges posed by the square relatively early in his career, especially when he played Jonathan Harker in the 1992 version of Bram Stoker's *Dracula*. The sextile between Neptune in Scorpio (vampires and other gloomy entities) and Pluto gave him with the opportunity to work with the dark forces highlighted by the squares in his chart. Throughout this production Reeves unwittingly embraced the rewards of this right-angled stellium that would turn on his inner light and help him to overcome his dyslexia.

So, when Reeves appeared in the first *Matrix* film in March 1999 his persona depicted an already honed and beautifully faceted personality free from any kind of learning disorder. It was, in my opinion, that through the *Matrix* trilogy that Reeves begin to shine as the glowing visionary he has frequently been depicted since.

For over a decade Reeves has also been a competent musician, playing guitar in the bands: Dogstar and Becky.[7] Once again, this technological and creative ability can be attributed to Uranus on the Ascendant squared to the MC; and Neptune endorsing it via its sextile to Uranus and the Ascendant.

Reeves had honoured the potential that constituted the purpose of the Counterpoints, especially the Sun and Mercury. Embracing the potential held within the Counterpoints[8] has helped him to *heal* via the stimulating challenges upheld by the square aspect.

Chart Data

Adele: May 5, 1988, 08:19 AM, Tottenham, North London, UK. Placidus system, mean Node.

Tom Hanks: July 9, 1956, 11:17 AM, Concord, California, USA. Placidus system, mean Node.

Keanu Reeves: September 2, 1964, 05:18 AM, Beirut, Lebanon. Placidus system, mean Node.

Endnotes

[1] The title given to her 2008 article that appeared in *The Mountain Astrologer* (TMA).

[2] Taken from Alan Oken's excellent publication *Soul Centred Astrology*.

[3] Alice A Bailey June 16 1880-December 15, 1949 wrote more than twenty-four books on theosophical subjects. Esoteric astrology became part of her Ageless Wisdom teachings, which she said was relayed to her by her Tibetan Master Djwhal Khul.

[4] The revelations of depression were made in an interview with *The Times* newspaper.

[5] Tom Hank's personal problems have been revealed recently in *Country Life* magazine.

[6] According to *Wikipedia* dyslexia is a reading disorder characterized by reading and general learning despite normal intelligence. Different people are affected in varying ways. Problems may include spelling words, reading quickly, writing words and sounding words in the head. Often these difficulties are noticed at school.

[7] Information source *Wikipedia*.

[8] Counterpoints represent problems with gifts attached to them.

Part Three
Prevention

"Examine the condition of the planets, whether in benevolent or malevolent signs; masculine or feminine, diurnal or nocturnal, hot, dry, cold or moist and part body they govern."—Nicholas Culpeper

Chapter 8

Evolutionary Memory

"If you tell the truth, you don't have to remember anything."—Samuel Clemens (Mark Twain)

Roy Cox, a research fellow at the Beth Israel Medical Centre in Boston and the Study's lead author, recently said: "The primary purpose of sleep is to selectively stabilize the emotional memories."

In this brief chapter we will be examining the effects of the memory modules known as the long and short-term memory—projections that emanate from the human brain. Also, we will be examining the metaphysical case histories that are projected via the evolutionary or astral memory—emanating from the spiritual heart or the soul.

The Musings of the Short-Term and the Long-Term Memory

It is generally perceived that the Moon has a powerful influence on the short-term memory. This is because the Moon's clement supremacy impacts upon the area of the brain known as the hippocampus (see diagram below). The short-term memory can be likened to a collection of alternating projections from a video camera, and because of the Moon's aqueous rulership the short-term memory can be attributed to the element of water, ebbing and flowing like the tides of the oceans.

In addition, the Moon is the planetary body that administers the human prerequisite for sleep, and purges the memories that are temporally held within the short-term or emotional memory.

When converging with the planet Pluto, the Moon shares a combined rulership over the long-term or psychological memory. Originally, the long-term memory was designed purely as a holding facility that projected images and memories from previous incarnations. Perhaps then, the long-term memory can be best described as a latent imaging system projecting near perfect images of the past, which are selected at random and which resonate perfectly with the moment. Pluto's long-term memory is intuitively and repeatedly drawn upon by dementia and Parkinson's disease sufferers.

Images recorded in the long-term memory are generally difficult to erase. This is because Pluto impacts upon the area of the brain known as the entorhinal cortex (the brain's central hard drive). However, Pluto is the planet that rarely relinquishes its grip on anything it considers to be poignant and non-negotiable. The entorhinal cortex represents a widespread network of deeply-engrained and often permanent memories (see diagram below).[1]

Scientifically speaking, the long-term memory represents a condensed form of light-enhanced imagery. Thus, Pluto evokes the projective states or latent images associated with this elemental form of imagery, and these projective conditions are in effect what the long-term memory symbolizes. Also, the long-term memory is connected directly to the evolutionary (spiritual) memory that has its rulership via Neptune.

More critically perhaps, the short-term and the long-term memory represent karmic storage devices—storing all our thoughts and events ready for play back in the life review once the physical life has been terminated.

The Evocations of the Evolutionary (Spiritual) Memory

The outer planets, including Jupiter and Saturn, are the cosmic catalysts that project images directly from the divine consciousness—characterizing our spiritual heritage. These divine images are the vital components that symbolize the spiritual or evolutionary memory that is contained within the soul or spiritual heart. And it is via the long-term memory (Pluto) that the evolutionary memory can be accessed.

Neptune has overall rulership of the spiritual memory[2]. Unfortunately, it is the spiritual memory that a large percentage of souls have blotted out, and why many misconceive the concept known as *God*. Accessing the evolutionary memory provides us with a feeling of bliss and hope. But because the populace can no longer tap into this source of remembrance, they prefer to delight in a temporary state of drug and alcohol induced bliss brought upon by Neptune. The relinquishing of the spiritual (evolutionary) memory is responsible, throughout the course of human evolution, for the onset of illness and disease.

In physicality, the spiritual memory remains housed firmly within the spiritual heart (the soul)—residing within the physical heart. However, according to the Akashic Records, the spiritual heart frequents the area between the left atrium and the right atrium at the exact centre of the human (physical) heart.

For this reason alone, it is vitally important to maintain the health of the physical heart. Therefore I recommend taking omega 3, 6, 7 and 9 as part of a healthy diet plan (refer to Chapter 10). This also maintains the wellbeing of the spiritual heart, which in effect, maximizes the potential of the physical heart.

Currently, in our fragmented societies, there is very little or no emphasis placed upon the spiritual heart. Re-embracing the spiritual memory substantially assists in the process of self-healing. Furthermore, embracing and evoking the energy of the spiritual heart, complete with its evolutionary memories, naturally raises the vibration of Neptune to the soul level, as advised by esoteric astrologers and practitioners.

The Heart Symbolism

According to the Akashic Records, the diamond shape on playing cards is the ancient and universal symbolism for the heart, *not* the traditional heart shape that we are mostly familiar with today (see diagram below).[3]

The combination of the emotional memory (the Moon), the psychological memory (Pluto) and the spiritual memory (Neptune), affects the twelve signs of the zodiac by denoting functional rationality and reason upon the brain and the heart, as detailed below:

The Four Qualities: Fire, Earth, Air and Water

Diagram 1, below, shows the functioning and circuitry connected proportions of the human brain—storing the short-term and long-term memories.

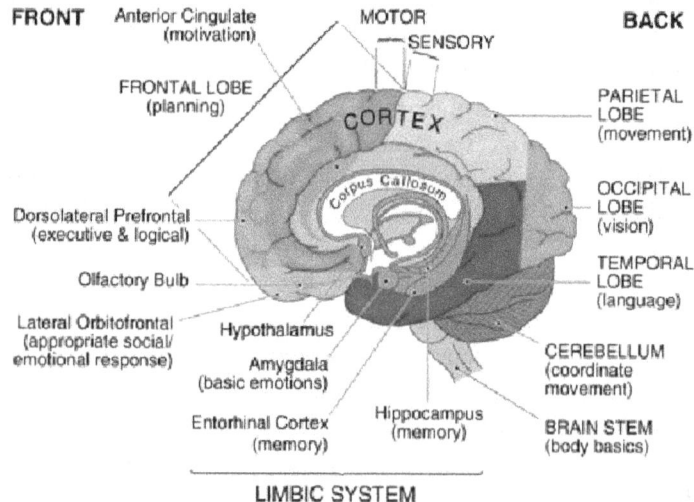

The Zodiacal and Planetary Rulers of the Limbic System

- Anterior Cingulate (motivation), Aries, Mars
- Frontal Lobe (planning), Virgo, Saturn[4]
- Dorsolateral Prefrontal (executive and logic), Capricorn, Saturn, Uranus
- Olfactory Bulb (visionary), Venus, Jupiter, Uranus, Neptune
- Lateral Orbitofrontal (social-emotional response), Libra, Cancer, Pluto
- Hypothalamus (reasoning), Taurus, Gemini
- Amygdala (base emotions), Moon, Pluto[5]
- Entorhinal Cortex (long-term memory function), Moon, Pluto[6]
- Hippocampus (short and long-term memory function), Moon, Pluto[7]
- Brain Stem (basic bodily responses), Aquarius, Leo Sun
- Cerebellum (coordination/movement), Mercury, Scorpio[8]
- Temporal Lobe (language), Mercury, Uranus, Gemini
- Occipital Lobe (vision), Neptune, Pisces
- Parietal Lobe (physical movement), Mercury, Virgo, Sagittarius
- Sensory Lobe (higher emotions), Moon, Cancer, Neptune, Pisces, Pluto
- Motor Lobe (cerebral function), Mars, Venus, Pluto

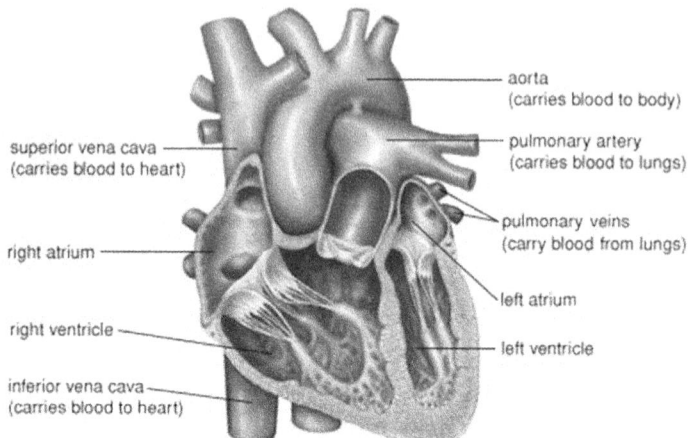

Diagram 2, above, shows the functioning and circuitry connected proportions of the human heart—storing the evolutionary (spiritual memory).

The Zodiacal and Planetary Rulers of the Cardiovascular System

- Aorta (blood circulation), Leo, Sun, Jupiter, Aquarius
- Pulmonary Artery (blood distribution to the lungs), Mercury, Gemini, Sagittarius, Uranus[51]
- Pulmonary Veins (blood retraction from lungs), Mercury, Virgo, Chiron, Mars.
- Left Atrium (blood filtration), Venus, Moon, Pluto, Scorpio
- Left Ventricle (blood pump), Saturn, Cancer, Sun, Aries
- Inferior Vena Cava (blood distribution to heart), Aquarius, Taurus, Libra, Moon
- Right Ventricle (blood pump), Neptune, Capricorn, Mars, Pisces
- Right Atrium (blood chamber), Mars, Pisces, Sun, Saturn
- Superior Vena Cava (blood distribution to heart), Sun, Uranus, Venus, Jupiter

Conclusion

In order to access the evolutionary memory the healing perception of positive thought (wellness) and stillness is recommended at all times throughout the course of the physical incarnation. Visualizing the violet and blue vibrations through meditation will also assist with entry into the domain of the spiritual memory.

Accessing the evolutionary memory will naturally maintain the short-term memory and purge the long-term memory of the deleterious energies associated with past events. I am not necessarily referring to *reminiscing* here. Rather I am referring to "holding on" to ills and grudges that are deposited within the confines of the long-term memory.

Remembering the creative potential held within the evolutionary memory will safeguard the body against the effects of illness and disease. What is not widely known is that the continual overloading of the long-term memory from past events has a toxic effect on the human brain, which in turn has consequences on the physical heart.

Dementia and Parkinson's disease are conditions that essentially render the victim into a permanent state of cerebral paralysis by which the long-term memory transmutes as the "life force"—effectively keeping the brain alive. Therefore, dementia is a relevant example of the toxic effects it instils upon the brain.

Endnotes

[1] Information source *Wikipedia*.
[2] In ancient mythology Neptune and Pluto were deemed as brothers.
[3] Information source the *Akashic Records*.
[4] The prefrontal node is the starting point for depression.
[5] The entorhinal cortex is the starting point for depression and dementia.

[6]The hippocampus is a starting point for depression and dementia.

[7]The cerebellum is the starting point for the onset of diabetes.

[8]The pulmonary artery represents an exacerbation point for the onset of diabetes; and the starting point for chronic heart disease.

Chapter 9

Sleep Deprivation

"Whether you think that you can, or that you can't,
you are usually right."—Henry Ford[1]

Sleep is the body's therapeutic medicine because it helps the body to heal from the stresses of the day. It is also an escape mechanism for the soul to return home to the spirit world for the purpose of healing, if only for a short time. Sleep deprivation deprives the soul of returning to its spiritual sanctuary in heaven—causing the onset of acute depression and other related psychological disorders. Therefore, sleep deprivation prevents self-healing.

The purpose of this significant inclusion is to bring to the forefront a bone of contention that has, over the last ten years, become a serious problem: sleep deprivation. Currently, sleep deprivation, or acute insomnia, is on the increase (especially throughout western civilization).[2]

Primarily, sleep deprivation is *congenital*, meaning that it is something that has occurred in a past life. However, sleep deprivation may also be the result of substandard diets, caffeine, and alcohol and drug addiction. In addition, it occurs because many constantly live life in the fast lane without applying the brakes. This way of life is tantamount to complete psychological and emotional meltdown. Unfortunately, these factors are all associated with modern-day living and invariably lead to the onset of illness and disease.

The problem is exacerbated by the increasing levels of obsession towards technological gadgets such as mobile phones, tablets and laptop computers, which in effect can cause sleep deprivation—leading to illness. Shockingly, the simple truth that many refuse to acknowledge is: if sleep deprivation becomes a consistent and perhaps a stringent factor in the life of an individual then physical and psychological decline is a certainty. At this point the body becomes the catalyst for the onset of psychological and physical illness.

Cosmic Catalysts

Sleep deprivation is an annoying factor, but it can become a dangerous characteristic detrimental to the health of any individual. Indentifying this potential dysfunction in the natal chart is however a relatively simple process. Sleep deprivation is highlighted when the Moon and Neptune are found in difficult alignment to each other; and if Saturn or Pluto are highlighted (linked to the Moon or Pluto via aspect) the condition is congenital. It may also be highlighted when these planets are not connected but receive hard aspects from other planets in the natal chart, especially from Mercury, Mars, and Uranus—borderline awakeners. Sleep deprivation is also likely to occur when there are hard aspects to planets frequenting the fourth and twelfth houses, especially if they lie at the midpoint of a critical pattern such as mutable T-Square or a Grand Cross.

In addition, temporary sleep deprivation (TSD) occurs when the Moon aligns with Neptune as a transiting opposition, quincunx or square; especially at the time of the full Moon. The effects of TSD are likely to affect individuals who are normally prone to acute insomnia, especially if stress levels are high, or the individual has consumed a significant amount of alcohol. Generally speaking though, the immediate effects from a Moon/Neptune transit will only be effective for around twenty-four hours, although it is widely accepted that the effects of this transit can produce insomnia for up to seven days after the initial alignment, particularly if the Moon was afflicted by other planets at the time. Also, if a Moon-Neptune transit occurs during the early hours it will likely disrupt the sleep patterns of an individual who is especially prone to the effects of insomnia.

Nasal and sinus problems can often become an issue during this particular transit, and it can also be the catalyst for the onset of a cold, particularly if Pisces is heavily tenanted. Flu-like and feverish symptoms can occur as a result of a Moon-Neptune transit, particularly if the immune system is heavily depleted from the likes of alcohol and caffeine. Nasal and sinus problems can also occur when the Moon aligns with Pluto as a frictional natal aspect in the birth chart.

If there are trines in addition to those hard aspects affecting the Moon or Neptune either natal or transit, then these will lessen the effects of sleep deprivation. However, the effects of the trine will be greatly influenced by the more dominant aspect such as the square. Theoretically, the trine will act as a *relaxant* that initially helps the body enter into REM deep sleep; the natural process that is disrupted by an afflicted Moon and Neptune.

Melatonin

The Moon and Neptune are closely connected to the pineal gland, and the pineal gland produces and secretes the hormone melatonin—necessary for the inducing of sleep at the physical level. Melatonin is secreted naturally into the brain when it gets dark in the evening—around nine or ten. Spiritually, the pineal gland is said to represent the third eye that projects the form of soul light energy, often viewed during meditation. Frictional aspects to the Moon and Neptune can also cause melatonin disruption, and in some cases melatonin dissemination (see next paragraph). Either way sleep deprivation occurs as a result. Individuals with frictional aspects between the Moon and Neptune are more likely to be what are termed as the "night owls."

Melatonin Disruption

Melatonin disruption can be detrimental to the general health of an individual especially if it occurs for long periods of time. According to the medical astrologer Wanda Sellar, "the pineal gland has been implicated in some disorders such as cancer, sexual dysfunction, hypertension, epilepsy, and Paget's disease (bone disorder)."

The continual absence of the hormone melatonin in the brain can inevitably lead to dementia, depression, epilepsy, psychosis, bi polar disorder, blindness and other more serious ailments such as tumours. Wanda Sellar also suggests that melatonin depletion can cause cancer. Sleep deprivation is the main perpetrator for narcolepsy. Narcolepsy sufferers frequently have the Moon or Neptune afflicted in the natal chart.

One example is highlighted in the plight of a friend of mine who suffers from this particular disease. In his natal chart the individual has an exact square between Mercury and Neptune, Mars and Uranus are in opposition, and the Moon links to Mars via semi-square—making this the pattern for the onset of this condition (see Eric's chart). Narcolepsy, like many other forms of illness causes melatonin disruption and health is significantly reduced as a result. In some cases where illness is prevalent, melatonin production has been categorized as non existent by GPs and medical and homeopathic practitioners.

Melatonin Dissemination

When dissemination occurs, the melatonin somehow becomes flushed through the body and out into the waste system. Dissemination often occurs when Pluto (waste) makes hard aspects to the Moon and Neptune and on occasion to Saturn. Disconcerting dreams and even nightmares that occur when the body doesn't reach REM sleep, are also a factor of melatonin disruption. This is because melatonin relaxes and calms the areas of the brain that trigger REM sleep (Rapid Eye Movement).

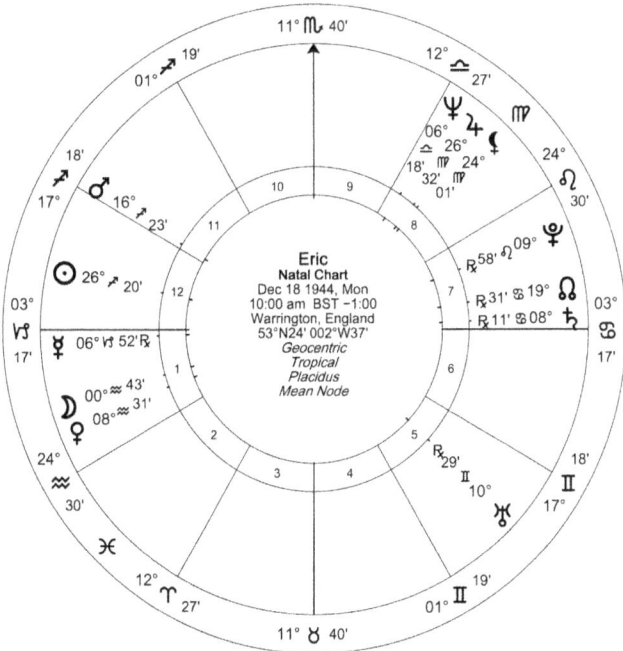

To alleviate sleep deprivation and melatonin distribution simply empower the body with violet, sapphire blue or silver light—whatever your personal and instinctive preference—and preferably via the visualization aspect technique suggested in Chapter 12, Guided Meditations. Regular practice of this technique will effectively improve sleep patterns greatly, increasing energy levels and momentum. In addition to this I would advise taking melatonin tablets. These supplements can also be included as part of the healthy diet plan. Melatonin supplements are widely available today and can be purchased from reputable suppliers (including Amazon).

Caffeine

An important point to consider in avoiding sleep deprivation is the inadvisability of consuming coffee after noon each day, because caffeine (a Neptune-ruled addictive stimulant) remains

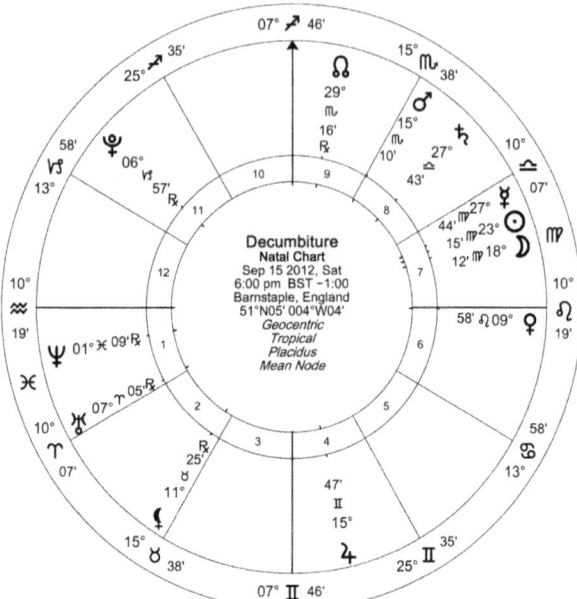

active in the blood stream for up to twelve hours. If consumed after noon caffeine can cause sleep disruption in one or two ways, and either way caffeine inhibits melatonin production.

Firstly, when caffeine remains in the blood stream the general pattern of sleep can be difficult to achieve, and if sleep is achieved the cycle frequently becomes fragmented and broken. This is attributed to having to visit the loo several times during the night. Sleep cycles are invariably broken because of disturbing dreams and as mentioned previously because of the frequent need to visit the loo. Often the need to visit the loo several times during the night can be the result of consuming caffeine after noon.

Many will be aware of the fact that there are small quantities of caffeine present in tea. Caffeine is essentially a diuretic (diuretic substances are ruled conjointly by Neptune and the Moon). As for the disturbing dreams, caffeine is a drug and therefore stimulates the dream receptors in the brain.

Alcohol

It is a well known fact that alcohol induces sleep, but only as a short-term measure. Once the body has metabolized the alcohol (generally speaking this is around four hours), the individual will find themselves wide awake because alcohol, like caffeine, acts as a stimulant and a diuretic. Heavy alcohol consumption, especially at night, can no doubt interfere with melatonin production, as alcohol *discombobulates* (agitates) the pineal gland.

The Biological Clock

This paragraph mostly applies to the residents of the United Kingdom. Sleep deprivation is also a consequence related to the changing of the clocks to British summertime. When the UK moves the clocks forward one hour around the end of March (just after the spring equinox) the biological (internal) clock can be seriously affected and as a result causes a range of health problems, including fatigue. Studies by the World Health Organisation, and in particular by Professor Russell Foster at Oxford University, have proven categorically that health issues arise as a result of this time-honoured tradition, which was originally intended to allow the farmers particularly in the UK an extra hour of light in order to retrieve their crops during the summertime.

Consequently, it takes the body around three weeks to realign the biological (circadian) clock to the imposing change. Those who are under the influence of a heavy Saturn transit (Saturn ruling time) at the time of the shift can be at most risk of incurring health problems. The circadian clock (under Saturn and Neptune's rulership) fine-tunes our physiology and behaviour to the demands of the cycle between light and dark. When it is interfered with, the results can often become fatal.

Sleep deprivation, as a result of this shift in the hour, has also been shown to increase [appetite], increasing our cravings for sugary products. And there can be additional consequences such as cancer, diabetes, and obesity, as a result of increased appetite and depression. With the correct amount of sleep the circadian clock will finally reset itself, though during the interim sleep deprivation can most definitely become a problem, especially when the Moon and Neptune align at the time of the alteration.

During the hour change that occurred in the small hours of March 26, 2017, the New Moon and Neptune were beginning to conjoin and both of these planets were squared to my natal Saturn in the twelfth house. It took me several days to recover from the effects extreme fatigue and energy depletion caused by sleep deprivation in the form of TSD.

Finally, when the clocks are altered again in the UK, at the end of October (moved backwards one hour), the effects are not as prevalent and far-reaching. This is because, in theory, the body gains an hour, as opposed to losing it. Obviously, this concept is an illusion (Neptune), but the body accepts it as so—triggering the notion that time, as demonstrated by the clock, is nothing but a circumspective illusion. The circadian clock is an intricate reflection of the chakras and the pineal gland, and thus its purpose is to make sure the soul is connected to its home in the spirit world.

Consuming melatonin supplements combined with Moon/Saturn and Neptune ruled vitamins and minerals (refer to Chapter 10) will help to alleviate symptoms associated with biological clock disruption. And if possible, surround your body with silver, blue and green rays via guided breath meditation (see Chapter 12).

Final Considerations

Paradoxically, when the Moon and Neptune align inharmoniously to other planets the opposite of sleep deprivation can occur. The afflicted individual can become entrenched in a cycle of sleeping too much. Sleeping more than nine hours a night is designated as "detrimental to the health" by the World Health Association primarily because it can cause conditions such as dementia, depression and anxiety disorder. Memory loss occurs when the brain contracts in size and too much sleep can cause this disadvantageous condition.

For the purpose of this publication we can refer to sleeping too much as "sleep acceleration" or SA; therefore I have noted that sleep acceleration can become an issue when the Moon and Neptune are afflicted to Mercury or Uranus and are also influenced (frictionally) by Saturn (contraction). For the purpose of this exercise let us briefly return to the natal chart of the narcolepsy sufferer. Here, it is interesting to note the individual in question has been beset by Alzheimer's dementia, diagnosed in 2012. Primarily, the point of diagnosis was when transiting Saturn conjoined Neptune, squared itself and afflicted Mercury via square. Also, in this chart Saturn squares Neptune and opposes Mercury as part of a t-square formation, which would clearly indicate sleep problems that are karmically induced in nature.

Common sense advice is necessary for maintaining good health and wellbeing. Today this is widely acknowledged, shared, and most importantly distributed by like-minded spiritual souls to those across the globe who yearn for change. If you seriously want to avoid sleep deprivation never consume coffee after noon, and definitely try to avoid consuming alcohol before bedtime.

Alternatively, if you want to avoid sleeping too much then I would recommend gentle exercise such as walking regularly, and possibly tai chi to be included into the daily routine. Also, try and reconnect with nature whenever possible, as this will help to balance the aural energy field. The excessive intake of sugar can have the opposite effect because sugar has always been designated as a stimulant and sugar transmutes into fat solids in the body. The poisoning effect can slow the body down, causing lethargy, which can lead to the onset of sleeping too much.

Chart Data

Eric: December 18, 1944, 10:00 AM, Warrington, Lancashire, England. Placidus system, mean Node.

Decumbiture: September 15, 2012, 18:00 PM, Barnstaple, Devon, England. Placidus system, mean Node.

Endnotes

[1] Henry Ford was the founder of the *Ford Motor Company*.
[2] Statistics courtesy of the *World Health Organization* (WHO).

Chapter 10

The Importance of Herbs, Vitamins and Minerals in the Natal Chart

"Things do not change;
we change."—Henry David Thoreau

Before I communicate my evaluation of the planetary effects upon nutrition, let me begin with a quote from the renowned physician, astrologer, botanist and herbalist Nicolas Culpeper. Continually criticising what he considered to be the unnatural methods of his contemporaries, Culpeper responded by saying:

"This not being pleasing, and less profitable to me, I consulted with my two brothers, DR. REASON and DR. EXPERIENCE, and took a voyage to visit my mother NATURE, by whose advice, together with the help of DR. DILIGENCE, I at last obtained my desire, and, being warned by DR. HONESTY, a stranger in our days, to publish it to the world, I have done it."[1]
Thus, *The Complete Herbal* was born!

The *Complete Herbal* by Nicolas Culpeper (1616-1654) listed herbs according to the diseases they relieved or cured. For example, the long-forgotten herb agrimony was good for liver complaints; Jupiter rules the liver, therefore, Jupiter rules agrimony. Each planet was designated as 'lord of a day' (Sun/Sunday, Moon/Monday, and so forth). Thus, herbs gathered on their planet's day, especially in the first and eight hours, were at their most efficient. Today, and perhaps more than ever, herbs are necessary components for the maintenance of good health.

The ancient spiritual premise of ingesting herbs in order to sustain good health remains both necessary and effective. But do try to purchase only organically grown herbs, especially when applying them as remedies for illness and disease. Culpeper's recommended herbal remedies (see below) are still available via reputable outlets.

Culpeper's Herbal Remedies, Adapted for the 21st Century

- Aries (Mars): Briony (purging, cramps, stitches); Crowfoot (drawing a blister); Honeysuckle (biliousness); Nettles (pleurisy, sore throat); Rhubarb (mild purgative); Capsicum (arthritis, cleaning blood). Ideally, to be gathered, or purchased, and consumed on Tuesdays.
- Taurus (Venus): Arrack (swelling of the throat); Beans (the water good for the complexion, half a bean will stop a cut and bleeding); Elder (root cures adder bite, flowers boiled, water calms sunburn); Lavender (wellness and calming); Hazel (tension); Milk thistle: silymarin, (relieves stress in the gallbladder). Ideally, to be gathered and consumed on Fridays.
- Gemini (Mercury): Carrot (helps conception); Fern (swollen spleen, makes ointment for cuts or prickles); Haresfoot (diarrhea and dysentery); Lavender (headache, toothache, fainting, apoplexy and dropsy). Ideally, to be gathered and consumed on Wednesdays.
- Cancer (Moon): Flax (inflammation, tumours, diseases of the chest and lungs); Privet (sore mouth, treating sores); Saxifrage (stomach weakness, cramps, convulsions, the leaves give a good flavour to wine); Slippery Elm (stomach

complaints); Wild Yam (menstrual cycle and hot sweats). Ideally, to be gathered and consumed on Mondays. Rosemary (preferably rosemary oil) to improve the memory. According to old wives tales lavender improves memory; this is wrong as lavender actually depletes memory.

- Leo (Sun): Bay (berries good for cold, rheumatism, expelling of wind); Celandine (piles and haemorrhoids); Walnuts and Pecans (pain and inflammation of the ears); Marigold, sometimes referred to as calendula, (wellbeing and cleaning the circulatory system); Lycopene (protecting the prostrate from disease). Ideally, to be gathered and consumed on Sundays.

- Virgo (Mercury with the possible inclusion of Chiron?): Caraway (helps digestion, fortifies the pancreas, sharpens the eyesight); Horehound (Chiron), (consumption, pain, yellow jaundice, gallstones particularly when Mars and Jupiter are prominent in the chart); Myrtle (prevents the spitting of blood, dysentery). Ideally, to be gathered and consumed on Wednesdays and Thursdays.

- Libra (Venus): Asparagus (expels kidney stone, stirring up lust); Chestnuts (bronchitis); Daisy (pleurisy and pneumonia); Garden Mint (hiccoughs, cleansing of the blood); Camomile and Almond Paste (relaxant, ideal for insomnia); Green Tea (cleansing the immune system). Ideally, to be gathered and consumed on Fridays.

- Scorpio (Pluto with the Possible Inclusion of Mars): Broom (clears the chest); Furze (jaundice, cleaning the kidneys); Hops (Mars, cleansing the blood, curing venereal disease, biliousness); Tobacco (rheumatic pain, toothache, powdered kills lice); Peppermint (fortifying the kidneys, indigestion). Ideally, to be gathered and consumed on Tuesdays and Fridays.

- Sagittarius (Jupiter): Betony (removes spots from face and hands); Borage (clarifies the blood, fortifies); Dandelion (cleans the urinary passages); Moss (eases inflammation);

Milk Thistle (fortifies the liver and gallbladder). Ideally, to be gathered and consumed on Thursdays.
- Capricorn (Saturn): Amaranthus (prevents bleeding); Beet (burns, weals, blisters); Hemlock (roasted, good for gout); Onion and Brazil Nuts (coughs, earache, increase sperm count); Garlic (colds, fevers and influenza); Lemon Blossom (arthritis, repairing joints); St. John's Wort (prevents Depression). Ideally, to be gathered and consumed on Saturdays.
- Aquarius (Uranus with the Possible Inclusion of Saturn): Heartsease (good for convulsions in children); Hemp (Saturn, expels the wind, but makes men sterile, kills worms); Medlar (prevents miscarriages); Quince (sore mouths). Ideally, to be gathered and consumed on Saturdays and Sundays.
- Pisces (Neptune and Jupiter): Dock (Jupiter, purging the blood, strengthens the liver, removes freckles, removes warts, chilblains); Sage (blackens the hair, cures headaches); Succory (drives forth cholera). Ideally, to be gathered and consumed on Wednesdays and Thursdays.

Always use the element of simplicity; human beings have become experts in the art of complication. Today, the harsh reality that everything has become unbelievably problematic is not only disturbing, but is accepted as normal. The above extracts from Culpeper's journals are a testament to the fact that the simplest explanation tends to be the right one (a scientific precept known as Occam's Razor).

Medical Astrology

Medical astrology, in all its diverse and unique forms, has become complicated because very rarely do we go back to basics in our interpretations. In addition, many in this field do not look to the planets as hierarchies—the rulers of all life and every aspect on Earth. To quote a fellow astrologer, "the planets rule everything."[2] However, we must not make the mistake of believing that the planets manipulate us; they merely influence us, but perhaps more importantly they reflect our current state of being.

Medical astrology is one such system that, in my experience witnessed throughout many quarters, has become unnecessarily complicated, even though it is much-needed for the prevention of illness and disease. Throughout our modern NHS, ignorance towards alternate therapies is common. Hippocrates said: "A physician without knowledge of astrology has no right to call himself a physician." Culpeper believed that simplicity and awareness were necessary elements in maintaining the body's health.

Culpeper attempted to make medical treatments more accessible to laypersons by educating them about maintaining their health. Ultimately, his ambition was to reform the system of medicine by questioning traditional methods and knowledge and exploring entirely new solutions for ill health. The systemisation of the use of herbals and minerals by Culpeper was a key development in the evolution of modern pharmaceuticals—most of which originally had herbal/mineral origins. Culpeper also associated illness and disease with planetary influences.

Currently, so many people are uneducated in the importance of correct nutrition, not viewing it as an essential element to perpetuating their health. Aside from the psychological profile, nutritional deficiency is one aspect why illnesses such as dementia, depression, psychosis, Parkinson's disease, Aids, insomnia, kidney disease and diabetes are distending. It is important to point out that all forms of illness and disease are not genetic, as popular consensus indicates. Illness and disease are caused by poor diet and stress, period!

Natal Aspects

Adverse aspects in the natal chart are responsible for vitamin and mineral deficiency, and most importantly for the onset of poor health. The signs that the planets tenant in a frictional aspect determine herbal deficiency. The type and strength of the aspect determines the level of deficiency. So, for example, when the Sun opposes Mars (an Antipathy), using no more than four degrees orb, there should always be an instinctive need present to strengthen the body's immune system. Providing of course that we are continually listening to our body's innate calling.

To overcome the nutritional deficient side of an adverse aspect we need to ingest the necessary vitamins and minerals that are categorised under their planetary rulerships (see table below). This will alleviate the problem of mineral deficiency in our diet, providing of course it exists in the first place.

The adverse planetary aspects that are responsible for vitamin and mineral deficiency are as follows: opposition, quincunx, sesquiquadrate, square and the conjunction. With the conjunction it depends on the planets concerned, as the conjunction can often be a neutral healing aspect.

If Mars and Saturn are conjunct then consider this alignment as one that is responsible for the onset of nutritional deficiency. A Sun-Venus (a Sympathy) conjunction however would be considered as moderate, and therefore the need to ingest the necessary minerals wouldn't necessarily be designated as urgent, although consuming the relevant minerals would still be recommended. T-squares, Grand Crosses and Yods (the double quincunx), etc. would need to be interpreted no differently, but merely as separate aspects.

Typically, quincunxes are very much an aspect to be wary of, especially in the form of the double inconjunction: the Yod.[3] On a physical level the quincunx indicates poor absorption and metabolization of nutrients; and it indicates an enormous appetite for the vitamin or mineral ruled by the planets in the aspect. Hence, a careful diet would have to be forged by a doctor, naturopath or dietician, particularly if any of the B vitamins are involved.

Peregrination

A further point of interest to pursue when diagnosing illness and disease in the natal chart is planets in peregrination; in other words planets that receive no major or Ptolemaic aspects from other planets. Peregrine planets are not capable of sharing or merging with other planets' energies and vibrations—peregrine planets simply cannot bounce off another planet as we might when in the company of a close friend or loving partner for example. This renders these planets vulnerable and susceptible to negative energies.

Moreover, planets in peregrination can be a source for concern where the potential onset of illness and disease is concerned, especially when retrograde.

Transits

Transiting planets to natal planets can equally have an immediate adverse effect on nutrition. With transits it is only the transiting planet that needs to be taken into consideration as this can often determine a level of deficiency in the body's current nutritional requirements. So, for example, if Neptune was transiting the natal Moon, the individual would need to begin taking or increasing the amount of omega 3 in the diet, along with other Neptune-ruled compounds, in order to guard against the onset of wasting illness. When Neptune transits the Moon, Saturn or Pluto, memory loss and the onset of dementia are likely scenarios.

Likewise, when two or more transiting planets are in aspect but are void of aspects to natal planets they exemplify severe nutritional deficiency at that particular time, especially when the planets transit the signs ruled by the luminaries. So for example, when Saturn transits Scorpio in a Scorpio Sun sign chart and the transiting Sun opposes Saturn stationed in Taurus, issues such as toothache or gum disease caused by receding gum lines and abbesses, would most likely be a concern because the body would ordinarily lack vital elements such as: vitamin E, vitamin D, magnesium and more importantly calcium. Of course the positions and aspects to the natal Sun and Saturn would also need to be considered for evaluation.

Under the influence of transits the body would always instinctively yearn for the foods that are rich in the vitamins and minerals ruled by the transiting planets. The effects of vitamin and mineral deficiency are increased when planets reach their counterpoint—natal and transiting— application and separation.

Here is a list of the most widely-publicised vitamins and minerals and their planetary rulers, including some of the known associated diseases.

The Planetary Index of Vitamins, Minerals and Additional Herbs:

According to Joel Wallach BS, DVM, ND and the founder of Youngevity, "the body needs 90 essential nutrients every day in order to be able to function to its optimum performance." Conversely, 90 essential nutrients (9 being Pluto's number in numerology) are also required in order that the physical body can successfully prevent the onset of illness and disease. However, for many this excess of combined supplementation would prove unattainable, simply because of the costly expense that is involved. I suggest listening to the wishes of the body in terms of what it requires with regards to vitamins, minerals and herbs— paying particular attention to herbs.

Throughout the following index of planetary rulerships are the essential nutrients listed individually. Also listed are their effects—effects that balance the natal chart and help implement complete physical, mental and spiritual wellbeing. The natal chart will determine what nutrients the body is deficient of, especially at times of adverse planetary activity. The index also includes essential herbs such as echinacea and nettle that instil calmness and composure:

Sun

- Magnesium—necessary for the prevention of IBS and diverticulitis and vital for sustaining a healthy immune system. Magnesium has been frequently referred to as the wonder mineral.
- Iodine (extracted mainly from seaweed)—necessary for the prevention of hair loss and problems associated with the nails. Iodine is also a liver and kidney cleanser, and should be taken at regular intervals if the patient has been diagnosed with a cystic liver.
- Vitamin A—necessary for the prevention of liver and kidney diseases such as hepatitis. Vitamin A also prevents jaundice (a yellowing of the skin and the pupils of the eyes), and even cancer.
- Vitamin D—aids in the prevention of depression and can help to alleviate conditions like Lyme disease. Commonly referred to as the sunshine vitamin. The ultra violet vibration harnessed from the Sun helps to eradicate cancerous cells in the body that have been enveloped by free radicals. It is also crucial for instilling wellness and maintaining a healthy equilibrium. Also, maintains a healthy circulation and aids in the prevention of bone diseases such as rickets. Vitamin D is perhaps the most important vitamin for maintaining a healthy immune system.
- Vitamin D is equally essential when taken in adolescence, as it can assist in the prevention of head lice and scalp problems, including dandruff (prone in adolescence). Traditionally, vitamin D is harnessed from the Sun, and its depletion is particularly noticeable around the crown chakra area; headaches, neuralgia, migraine and cerebral tension are telltale symptoms of vitamin D depletion. Although vitamin D is absorbed through the skin it is through the scalp that vitamin D is more commonly absorbed before it is released into the rest of the body and into the organs.

- Coenzyme Q10— although not officially deemed as a vitamin or mineral it is nevertheless an excellent and vital addition especially when it comes to replenishing energy levels in later life (mainly after 60). Coenzyme Q10 is a master energy boost for preventing illness and disease, and essential for maintaining a healthy heart, skin and circulatory system.
- Salt (preferably obtained in good quality form) is recommended, especially moist locally sourced sea salt, or Pink Himalayan mountain salt, which is best, providing it is easily obtained. Despite majority opinion to the contrary, salt is perhaps the most crucial of all the minerals because it is constantly secreted through the skin cells. Salt is required in order to prevent the likes of muscle cramps, poor circulation and insomnia. Additional salt consumption in the diet is vital if the Sun and Saturn are squared or quincunxed, or form the sextile as part of a Yod configuration in the natal chart. When the Sun and Saturn are afflicted the body tends to lose large amounts of salt through adverse and even undetected perspiration via the joints and nervous complaints.
- Salt is a vital component for the production of hydrochloric acid, stored in the stomach, and indispensable for healthy food digestion. If the Sun is afflicted in the chart an imbalance of hydrochloric acid can frequently occur. When the body produces too much acid, reflux can occur; and in the worst case scenario 'hydrochloric acid saturation' can lead to the onset of a hiatus hernia. In addition, tests have revealed that a depletion of salt in the diet can lead to the onset of dementia, depression and diabetes. The Sun shares its rulership of salt with Saturn (more about salt further on). Acid reflux occurs when the Sun, Mars, Saturn, Uranus and Neptune are afflicted in the natal chart.
- Lycopene, a carotenoid, is an essential nutrient contained in tomatoes and all red vegetables including beetroot (a

Saturn-ruled vegetable). It is a powerful nutrient that promotes healthy living. Tomatoes belong to the poisonous deadly nightshade genus (Neptune ruled plants); therefore it is imperative that they should be cooked before consuming in order to neutralize the moderate amounts of poison contained in this super fruit. Once cooked the lycopene in tomatoes is released and is absorbed and metabolized far easier in the body than when consumed raw.

- Lycopene reacts to heat. This is determined by the rich red color of the cooked tomato. The consumption of Sun-dried tomatoes is perhaps one of the best ways of attaining lycopene, as they have harnessed the healing power and vitamin D released by the Sun. I have always believed that the Mediterranean diet is an important consideration when it comes to maintaining good health. Regular consumption of lycopene can act as prevention against dementia and depression. It also helps the body guard against prostrate, bladder, breast and urinary tract cancer. Prostrate cancer is often identified in a male chart when the Sun and Pluto are in square formation, inconjunct or in opposition. Likewise, breast cancer is often identified when the Sun, Jupiter, Saturn or Pluto afflicts the Moon in a female chart.
- The Earth Influence: The Earth is always positioned in the natal chart in an exact 180 degree opposition to the Sun. Therefore, I would suggest that the Sun ruled vitamins and minerals (particularly magnesium) are continually integrated into a healthy and sustained diet in order to support the immune system. Both the luminaries and Saturn are the planets that are the primary rulers of the immune system.

Moon

- Potassium—the short-term memory improver—necessary for the prevention of dementia, depression and insomnia.
- Vitamin B2, Riboflavin, necessary for the prevention of scabies, and for the prevention of sinus infections because

the Moon rules the mucus membranes. Nasal drip caused by sinus infections depletes the immune system.
- Omega 3 fatty acid, found in mackerel, sardines, anchovies, mullet, snapper, tuna and krill (all Moon-ruled fish). Omega 3 is vital for strengthening the immune system and helps to prevent furring and hardening of the arteries. It also helps to keep the blood thin and supports the immune system. Interestingly, the omega fatty acids are not produced in the body, so it is crucial that they are included as part of a healthy diet plan.
- The miracle healing power of blueberries and bilberries: blueberries and bilberries are extremely high in lunar antioxidants, and therefore vital for boosting the mood. These can be attained via supplement form.
- It has been proven at the Centre for Addiction and Mental Health in Toronto Canada that these miracle berries can neutralize the effects of manic depression, anxiety disorder and post natal depression. Saturn (the Moon's polarity planet) has the potential to instil depression and anxiety; therefore his opposite feminine polarized influence in the cosmos has the potential to heal these mental dis-eases. Blueberries are particularly delicious when consumed as a smoothie, the modern-day expression for a highly-nutritional blended commodity drink.
- An Important Fact: Recently it has come to my attention (mainly through my consultations) that a high percentage of people ingest vitamins and minerals with hot fluids, such as tea and coffee. Vitamins and minerals should only ever be taken with cold water, preferably mineral or distilled water. Unfortunately, hot fluids will neutralize the effects of the supplements, especially vitamin C and D. In some cases oesophageal damage has occurred particularly with capsule-based supplements. Hot fluids, such as tea and coffee (particularly strong coffee that also renders the vitamin or mineral deficient), quickly dissolves the gelatine

shell of the capsule thus dissolving it long before it reaches the stomach; therefore the contents sticks to the wall of the oesophagus causing irritation and even thinning of this delicate part of the body causing cancer. Through research into this particular study I have discovered those individuals with the Moon conjunct Mars, or when the Moon links to Mars via a frictional aspect such as the square, are more likely to take food supplements with hot fluids.

Mercury

- Vitamin B1, Thiamine is necessary for the prevention of beriberi — a degenerative nervous disorder.
- Lecithin, a mineral that is co-ruled by Mercury and Pluto, is referred to as the *brainy* mineral. It also helps to protect the myelin sheath from degeneration (this is the soft fatty tissue that forms around certain nerve fibres in the body). Regular consumption of lecithin can also help to reduce the symptoms of ear problems like tinnitus. Consumed regularly, lecithin guards against the onset of dementia, depression, anxiety, bipolar, narcolepsy and insomnia. Lecithin depletion is indicated in the natal chart via Mercury-Pluto squares, inconjunctions and oppositions. Interestingly, thiamine helps the body produce lecithin naturally.
- Mercury is the "messenger," carrying and distributing vitamin D to all the major organs in the body (the immune system).
- Nettle supplements, traditionally used as a prevention for all types of disorders associated with the nerves, such as Alzheimer's disease, Multiple sclerosis, Huntingdon's disease and Parkinson's disease. Nettle leaves contain high levels of protein, calcium, phosphorus, iron, magnesium, beta-carotene, vitamins A, C and D and the B complex. Nettle has been evaluated by the World Health Organisation for its antioxidant properties and its resistance towards microorganisms, and other more serious bacterial diseases such as

Escherichia coli (food poisoning) and Neisseria meningitides (meningitis). Microorganisms (fungi) are also associated with Pluto, particularly Neisseria gonorrhoea (sexually transmitted gonorrhoea).
- Ginkgo Biloba is necessary to maintain normal cognitive functions within the body. Ginkgo biloba is the most commonly ingested herb for brain health. Studies also show Ginkgo to improve the circulation to the extremities including the brain, and has been shown to improve memory in the short-term.

Venus

- Vitamin B3, Niacin, is necessary for the prevention of Bell's palsy and diseases of the inner ear such as labyrinthitis (a form of vertigo).
- Copper is necessary for the prevention of jaundice, intestinal disorders, skin eruptions, measles, rubella and diabetes. Both copper, found in apricots, and vitamin E, found in avocados (both are Venus ruled fruit), balance the Mars ruled mineral iron and are therefore most effective when ingested together.
- Vitamin E is necessary for the prevention of depression and skin ailments. Also, assists in the prevention and cure of the major throat disorders such as: tonsillitis, laryngitis and quinsy's. Eating avocados as part of healthy diet can also help to prevent throat cancer.
- Plant Sterols have been traditionally prepared throughout times gone by to guard against fatty acid deposits (cholesterol) from forming in the blood. Also, plant sterols act as blood purifiers, filtering the blood of toxins.
- Bromelain is a natural enzyme extracted mostly from pineapples. A natural remedy that helps the body guard against the onset of osteoporosis and rheumatoid arthritis. Good for the joints, particularly the knees.
- Peppermint Oil is traditionally used for its carminative and

spasmalytic effect on the digestive system, which is the primary element when listed under the rulership of Venus. Peppermint oil is also listed under Pluto.
- Silymarin (Milk Thistle) is necessary for healthy gallbladder and liver function, and relieves the effects of indigestion caused by overeating.
- Plant antioxidants (available from reputable suppliers) are necessary for balancing and maintaining the immune system, particularly the digestive track. In addition, they assist the body improve its oxygen absorption. Plant antioxidants are comprised of extracts of green tea, grape seed, rosemary and oregano. Plant antioxidants are often known as ORAC (Oxygen Radical Absorption Capacity). This is a measurement used in the method of measuring antioxidant capacities in foods.

Mars
- Iron is necessary for the prevention of anaemia and other blood disorders. Also, iron helps to prevent the total loss of hearing, especially in later life, and other disorders of the ear such as labyrinthitis (inflammation of the inner ear). Hearing loss caused by iron depletion is particularly prevalent in women who have experienced problems in childbirth or have undergone hysterectomies. This is because these types of traumas cause an imbalance in the natural Venus-Mars polarity, masculine and feminine energy.
- Phosphorus is necessary for helping to metabolize vital food deposits into the small intestine.
- Selenium is necessary for the prevention of lung disease, cancer and dementia and sepsis, which is a Mars-Saturn condition.
- Sodium is necessary for the prevention of stomach ailments and digestive upsets. A depletion of sodium can also lead to the onset of nervous disorders.
- Chlorine is a stomach cleanser; used primarily for the pre-

vention of colds and influenza.
- Folic Acid is necessary for helping to multiply and sustain the red blood cells in the body.
- Vitamin B12 is assists with the multiplying of white blood cells in the body.
- Cucumin, the main element found in Turmeric, is particularly effective in the prevention of blood cancers such as myeloma. Turmeric is also effective against joint degeneration.

Jupiter

- Zinc is necessary for the prevention of dementia, depression and insomnia. Zinc depletion in the body can lead to other serious afflictions such as hepatitis. Hepatitis B is transmitted via blood transfusions—blood that is diseased—and especially when depleted of zinc. Zinc depletion is indicated by hard aspects to Jupiter, especially when received from hazy Neptune.
- Manganese assists in warding off lice, and coupled with vitamin D can help to cure Lyme disease caused by tick bites.
- Biotin (vitamin H) is necessary for the prevention of cirrhosis of the liver.
- Chromium is necessary as an additional boost for the immune system.
- Vitamin B6 is necessary for the production of healthy bile, especially in the liver's storage compartment, the gallbladder. Vitamin B6 is necessary for the well-being of the pancreas and helps to guard the pancreas against cancer.
- Flaxseed Oil and Sea Buckthorn Berry Oil are the vegan or vegetarian alternative to the omega fish-based oils. Rich in Omega 3, 6, 7 and omega 9 fatty acids (omega 7 is Sea Buck Flower only). Flaxseed Oil is particularly effective in maintaining skin, hair and nails, and is also recommended for a healthy heart.

Saturn
- Bioflavonoids (citrin , vitamin P) strengthens and rejuvenates the body's immune system and guards against dis-eases such as lupus.
- Vitamin C, known widely as the miracle vitamin for its benefits, which are quaquaversal, meaning that the effects of vitamin C are pinpointed all over the body. Vitamin C is a powerful antioxidant, meaning that it attacks free radicals (antibodies) in the bloodstream. The main antioxidants characterized as dietary are: Vitamin A, C and E, ruled conjointly by Jupiter, Saturn and Venus—a powerful combination.
- Echinacea (named purple coneflower) is recommended for the prevention and relief of influenza and other cold-based dis-eases. Consuming Echinacea is strongly advised if there is a history of cancer within the family unit, particularly colon and oesophageal cancer. The flowers from the Echinacea plant render free radical (malignant) cells inoperable,; and the enzymes found in the purple flowers strengthen the body's immune system.
- The purple (Jupiter-Pluto) vibration is the antioxidant vibration, and assists with the production of serotonin in the gut.[4] Dietary antioxidants are perhaps best found in purple fruit and vegetables. Purple fruit and vegetables are rich in vitamins A, C and E and anthocyanin. Anthocyanin is essentially a plant compound, a type of bioflavonoid; therefore this compound comes under the rulership of Saturn. The purple coloration nourishes the organs, cleanses the blood, energises the chakras and purges the soul. The color purple strengthens the immune system; and in layman's terms the immune system symbolizes the inner skin (Saturn), protecting the organs.
- Recommended fruit and vegetables are as follows: blackberries, blueberries, blackcurrants, bilberries, elderberries, purple grapes, plums, prunes, dried raisins, purple

asparagus, purple cabbage, eggplant, purple carrots, beet, purple potatoes, purple peppers and purple cauliflower—all containing Jupiter, Saturn, Pluto vibrations—Jupiter ruling the purple vibration and the plants growth above the ground, Saturn ruling the Bioflavonoids and the plants stems or spines, and Pluto, also ruling the purple vibration and the plants support below the ground (roots, etc.).

- Dietary antioxidants, when taken at regular intervals, assist in the prevention of every known illness and disease. On its own, vitamin C protects the body's normal cells from being compromised or enveloped by free radicals and cancerous (dis-eased) cells. Also, vitamin C, combined with zinc (its polarity vitamin) and selenium repairs damaged skin cells, especially cells that have been damaged by excessive sunburn.
- Vitamin K is necessary for the prevention of blood clots in the brain and the heart. Vitamin K helps the body guard against the onset of Cardiovascular Accidents (strokes), making Vitamin K an essential part of a healthy diet plan. An afflicted Saturn in the natal chart exemplifies vitamin K deficiency. Avocado pears are a good source of nutrition and vitamin K.
- Calcium is necessary for the prevention of brittle bone disorder and joint disorders. Large doses of calcium and magnesium can help to prevent diseases such as Hurler's syndrome.[5] Also, vital for the prevention of fungus that grows on the toenails and on the fingernails. Calcium is said to aid the body when fighting off thrush, especially in women. It is important to remember however that calcium is better absorbed into the body when taken with magnesium,—its polarity mineral.
- Sun-Saturn harmonious alignments such as trines indicate that calcium is naturally maintained in the body and therefore a lesser dose is required daily in order to bolster the immune system. What this means is that the nutritional

effects of calcium remain in the body much longer with a trine as opposed to the square or opposition, where it is inclined to leach from the body via the urine.
- Sulphur is necessary for the prevention of pancreatic cancer, gout and especially diabetes.
- Vanadium is necessary for the prevention of skin and bone cancer and dementia.
- Cacao (extracted from the bitter coco bean) is coco in its purest form. This nutrient is necessary for healthy circulation by maintaining the flow of blood around the body. Cacao is also a powerful antioxidant and is helpful in reducing fatigue and stress.
- Quercetin (a class of water-soluble plant pigments called flavonoids). can be found in onions, apples and green and black tea. It is necessary for the neutralization of free radicals, therefore reducing the potential harm to cells.
- Pycnogenol, a unique flavonoid extracted from the bark of the maritime pine, is a powerful antioxidant necessary to protect and rebuild the body's collagen. It also supports the body's circulation.
- Salt is under Saturn's rulership. High doses of salt consumption assist in the prevention of some of the most intrusive and prolific dis-eases of the twenty-first century such as dementia, depression and diabetes. Also, an increased level of salt in the diet is an ideal preventative for cellulites and gout. Moreover, salt, under Saturn's rulership, assists in the building of a strong and healthy bone structure (skeletal system). Salt must always be an essential part of the diet if the Sun and Saturn are conjunct or opposition in the natal chart.
- Saturn, it is widely believed, stabilizes and strengthens the immune system, especially when large doses of vitamin C are applied in conjunction with salt. Vitamin C is particularly effective when lung diseases, such as emphysema

and sarciodosis, have been potentially treated with steroids (steroids prevent the immune system from attacking the vital organs). As a further point of interest, vitamin C is absorbed more effectively when there is a sufficient amount of zinc and selenium in the body.
- This balanced combination of elements (coupled with good quality salt) builds a strong resistance to diseases such as sepsis, measles and prostate cancer in men. Furthermore, the combination of vitamin C, zinc, zinc being the polarity of vitamin C, selenium and salt, the polarity mineral of selenium, maintains the correct healthy balance of hydrochloric acid in the stomach, also necessary for a strong immune system.

Uranus

- Genetically modified vitamins and minerals that are now in circulation. This type of supplement can either be supportive or damaging to the immune system, depending chiefly on how it has been manufactured. Always check out the suppliers.
- Also, some wheat grass supplements have been proven to assist in the alleviation of muscle contractions, spasms and convulsions; particularly the spasm-like fits concerned with epilepsy (a typically Uranus condition). Wheat grass is also a good remedy when used in the prevention of acute anxiety disorder and related dis-eases such as psychosis, schizophrenia, autism, bipolar disorder and depression. Wheat grass supplements are particularly good for counteracting the side-effects of alcohol, particularly dehydration caused by the overconsumption of gluten-based beers.
- **An Important Note about the Potentially Damaging Side Effects of Uranus and Technology:** When Uranus is afflicted in the natal chart via transit, or transit Uranus to another planet, the overuse of technological gadgets such as computers and particularly mobile phones will deplete the

body's immune system. A depleted immune system will inevitably lead to illness and disease; and in particular the onset of mental health problems such as anxiety disorder and psychosis. So, when one is under the influence of a frictional Uranus transit, the overuse of technology is applied in an instinctive manner, meaning that we naturally reach for our gadgets more than usual. Teenagers are particularly susceptible to the effects of Uranus, particularly when the overuse of computer games such as Xbox is apparent.

- Because Uranus has co rulership with Neptune over the body's hypersphere (the aura), the radioactive energy waves emitted from mobile phones and other forms of technology will interfere with the magnetic frequency generated by the body's aura, causing interference that is often detrimental to health. Teenagers, in particular, can develop ADHD (Attention Deficit Hyperactive Disorder covered in Chapter 4); and epilepsy (both of which are Uranus disorders), because of a compromised aural energy field caused by the frequent use of computers and mobile phones. Epilepsy can manifest because of certain conditions and not always as a genetic condition.

- I would recommend that during planetary cycles when Uranus is afflicted, paying particular attention to the presence of Mars, Saturn and Neptune transits (especially when these planets have reached their Counterpoint with Uranus); the use of technology should be restricted until such time it is deemed as safe. In other words at such time when the transit has culminated.

- As all transit cycles are meant to be a time of healing and contemplation it would be advisable not to consider returning to the old way of doing something, hence the old habits. It has now been confirmed that the overuse of mobile phones should be avoided because of the dangers poised by these gadgets. For example, the overuse of smart phones is responsible for the formation of tumours in the

- brain (Uranus), cysts and insomnia, which is detrimental to overall health in the long term (see Chapter 12 for more information about sleep deprivation).
- I am not implying that we should give up our enjoyment and use of technology, I am merely advising the use of caution here. For example, text rather than phone a friend, and instead of saying 'one more game'. call it a night instead.
- To aid the immune system during transitory cycles to Uranus daily doses of the Sun-ruled mineral magnesium and vitamin D will assist in the prevention of immune system depletion. Also, the Saturn-ruled mineral calcium is required in order to further enhance the immune system. And I would recommend the Mercury-ruled mineral lecithin as an immune boost.
- Finally, it is important to emphasize that when a planet is under stress in the chart, whether natal or transiting, it is advisable to include within a healthy diet plan the vitamins and minerals ruled by its polarity planet; in this example it is the Sun. According to Dr. Robert Jansky in his excellent book *Astrology and Nutrition*, 'it is important that we take the vitamins, minerals and tissue salts that fall under the rulership of the polarity planet of our Sun sign.' This is a notion I fully endorse.

Neptune

- Omega 6 and 9 fatty acids (perhaps the most crucial in the Omega family of fatty acids—found primarily in deep water inhabiting species such as sole and turbot—necessary for the prevention of organ failure. It is crucial for the maintenance of the heart and kidneys, and can help to prevent the onset of dementia, depression and diabetes. The Omega fatty acids are necessary for the lubrication of the joints such as the knees and the wrists. Repetitive strain injury and particularly carpal tunnel syndrome affecting the hands and wrists is a direct result of Omega fatty acid depletion.

- Pantothenic Acid (Calcium Pantothenate, or vitamin B5) is necessary for the prevention of tiredness and fatigue, and all major skin diseases, such as eczema, dermatitis, ringworm and shingles. Calcium Pantothenate is particularly effective against epilepsy. When taken regularly it helps to decrease the amount and the severity of epileptic seizures. Also, Calcium Pantothenate helps to guard against the effects associated with physical and intellectual biorhythm depletion.
- Vitamin B17, found in apricot kernels (the core of the apricot), which are poisonous in large quantities, is a powerful immune system support and cleanser, particularly effective in the prevention of rubella, measles, scarlet fever, mumps, tetanus, typhoid and chicken pox. The lower vibration of Neptune (Venus) rules the flesh or the fruit of the apricot. Unfortunately, apricot kernels may not be available in some countries such as the USA, in which case an alternate source of vitamin B17 can be sourced from sunflower seeds and rapeseed. Small traces of this vitamin have previously been detected in these nutritious and protein-enriched food sources.
- Misdiagnosis is attributed to Neptune. This will only occur when the body is out of synchronization. For example, when the content of alcohol is high in the bloodstream, or when the body is beset by drug abuse. The presence of these illusionary substances places an invisible shield around the body that interferes with technology and somehow with human diagnosis. In this hi-tech world the misdiagnosis of mental health disorders is on the increase. One example is Asperger's Syndrome, which is often misdiagnosed as ADHD.

Pluto

- Boron, an element found in diamonds, ruled by Mars (the lower vibration of Pluto), supports and assists with the

healing of the immune system, and is the vital element responsible for the reproduction of the red blood cells. Boron can help to cure herpes (a venereal disease). Notably, boron is the element symbolizing rebirth.
- Fluorine is necessary for the prevention of bowel-related diseases such as diverticulitis and Crohn's disease. In some cases fluorine-based compounds can act as a laxative for the treatment of constipation. Fluorine can also help to repair the intestinal villi damaged by the overconsumption of gluten-based products containing the gluten enriched grains: wheat, rye, oats and barley.
- Lecithin, as the long-term memory improver, is necessary for the prevention of dementia, depression, insomnia and narcolepsy. Lecithin (taken at regular intervals) also guards against spinal degradation and particularly leukaemia. It is essential to take lecithin if Mercury and Pluto are linked via hard aspect such as a square or opposition in the natal chart.
- Saw Palmetto (an ancient and powerful plant sterol) is a concentrated extract from the berries of the saw palmetto palm tree. Traditionally used as a prevention for prostrate cancer and other related problems in men, it is advisable that men begin taking this supplement around 50 years of age.
- Peppermint Oil is traditionally used for its carminative and spasmalytic effect on the digestive system. Under Pluto's rulership, peppermint oil is particularly effective in reducing the burning effects associated with acid regurgitation caused by hiatus hernias. However, to counteract the effects of acid regurgitation peppermint oil needs to be taken at regular intervals. Also, I suggest that it is only purchased from reputable suppliers and is completely organic in origin. Most inorganic peppermint oils tend to be rancid.
- Hiatus hernias are often the result of drinking fluids when

eating food—particularly food that is high in fat content. Mixing fluids with solids creates stress in the stomach and digestive tracts. I always recommend that eating and drinking are kept separate, or at least within one hour of consuming either. This applies particularly to people with the Moon in hard aspect to Saturn, Neptune and Pluto.

Essential Vitamin Deficiency, Pivotal Functions

In this directory are some of the common afflictions caused by vitamin and mineral deficiency. These afflictions are caused mostly by transiting planets. So for example, the onset of a particular allergy would be caused by vitamin C deficiency and transiting Saturn would most likely be the culprit here, especially to natal Venus or Neptune.

- Vitamin A: Eye problems, poor eye sight, poor night vision, poor hearing, loss of smell, spots, dry flaky skin, oily skin, dandruff, mouth ulcers, throat infections, colds, diarrhoea, stuffy nose, nausea, depression, insomnia, warts, thrush, cystitis, sties, fatigue and loss of appetite.
- Vitamin C: Colds, lack of energy, infections, allergies, wrinkles, sagging skin, poor lactation, poor digestion, bleeding gums, dental cavities, bruising, nose bleeds, slow wound healing and anaemia.
- Vitamin D: Rheumatism, rickets, middle backache, muscle spasm, lack of energy, tooth decay, hair loss, coarse hair, dry skin, nearsightedness, chilblains and weight problems.
- Vitamin E: Loss of sex drive, dry skin, excess sweating, exhaustion after gentle exercise, easily bruised, infertility, varicose veins, oedema and puffy ankles.
- Vitamin K: Brittle bones, arthritis, joint problems, imbalances in the blood, excess clotting, type 2 diabetes, kidney disease and blocked arteries.
- Complete Vitamin B Complex, Working in Synergy: Confusion, irritability, depression, insomnia, hair loss,

premature grey hair, acne, bad skin, poor appetite, insomnia, neuritis, tension, difficulty relaxing, constipation, and sleepiness after meals, dementia, allergies and hay fever.
- Vitamin B-1: Tender muscles, stomach pains, constipation, prickly sensations in the legs, eye pains and type 2 and type 1 diabetes.
- Vitamin B-2: Bloodshot and itchy eyes, burning and gritty eyes, sore tongue, cracked lips, cataracts, eczema, dull oily hair, split nails, trembling, sluggishness and dizziness.
- Vitamin B-3: Fearfulness, fatigue, acne, headaches, loss of appetite, migraines, bad breath, skin eruptions, insomnia, irritability, tender gums, depression, rough inflamed skin, tremors, allergies, loss of memory, dementia and a coated tongue.
- Vitamin B-5: Apathy, abdominal pains, restlessness, vomiting, asthma, allergies, burning feet, muscle cramps and exhaustion.
- Vitamin B-6: Irritability, water retention, bloatedness, depression, loss of hair, cracks around mouth and eyes, numbness, cramps in legs and arms, slow learning, morning sickness, post natal depression, allergies, nervousness, tingling hands and menopausal arthritis.

Essential Nutrient Deficiency, Pivotal Functions Continued

- Boron: The essential brain nourishing mineral because in balanced doses boron guards against dementia and depression. Boron enhances brain function, eye-hand coordination, short-term memory and boosts the body's level of concentration.
- Calcium: Calcium is a mineral that is essential for the correct function of the body's immune system. It maintains the bones and teeth and helps to maintain the body's heart rhythm. The mineral is also required for muscle contrac-

tions and relaxation, nerve and hormone function, and blood pressure regulation. Long-term calcium deficiency is also responsible for the onset of depression and insomnia.
- Copper: Reduced thyroid function, cardiovascular disease, high blood pressure, increased uric levels, increased cholesterol, depression, impaired glucose tolerance, bone defects and dementia.
- Iron: Anaemia, extreme fatigue, pallor, hair loss, irritability, impaired immune function, type 2 and type 1 diabetes, depression, kidney disease and painful tongue and weakness.
- Magnesium: Magnesium is by far the most important mineral. Alarmingly, 78 percent of people in the world are magnesium deficient. According to Dr Sidney Baker,[58] "Magnesium deficiency can affect virtually every organ system in the body with regard to skeletal muscle, one may experience twitches, cramps, muscle tension, muscle soreness, including back aches, neck pain, tension headaches and jaw joint (or TMJ) dysfunction, also magnesium deficiency can lead to the onset of dementia and diabetes and kidney disease. Also, one may experience chest tightness or a peculiar sensation that he can't take a deep breath. Sometimes a person may sigh a lot."
- Potassium: Abdominal pains, palpitations, low blood pressure, tingling, weakness in arms, type 2 and type 1 diabetes, depression, insomnia, kidney disease, hallucinations, extreme fatigue and nausea.
- Selenium: Excess lethargy, hypothyroidism, mental fatigue and depression, insomnia, reproductive disorders; in some cases women have miscarried because of selenium deficiency. Long-term selenium deficiency has also been contributed to the onset of dementia.
- Zinc: Chronic liver disease and chronic kidney disease, muscle cramps, Crohn's disease, sickle cell disease, growth

restriction, macular degeneration, impaired wound healing, type 2 and type 1 diabetes, depression, insomnia, dementia, kidney disease and weight loss.

Conclusion

Correct nutrition feeds the higher aspects of the psyche and realigns the soul with the divine consciousness. Healthy nutrition harmonizes the physical and physiological bodies with the spiritual body. Therefore, good nutrition is essential for self-healing.

[1] A quote from Culpeper's medical journals.

[2] A quotation profoundly imparted by the astrologer Betty Gosling.

[3] Yods, quincunxes and semi-sextiles (inconjuncts) are frequently overlooked in the natal chart. A Yod is also known as the Finger of Fate or the Finger of God. This is because Yod, which looks like the astrological yod glyph, is the tenth Hebrew letter with significant Kabbalistic and mystical significance regarding the name of God, his omnipresence and our humility.

[4] Serotonin is the 'feel good' enzyme. It helps to reduce anxiety and depression, so if we fill our stomachs with unhealthy food effectively the serotonin will be contaminated and have a detrimental effect on the body. Consuming healthy food will not only keep us free of illness and disease but chemically-balanced serotonin will help us to achieve good quality sleep. I would recommend reading *The Happy Kitchen* by Rachael Kelley in order to learn more about the importance of serotonin produced by a healthy and nutritious diet.

[5] Hurler's syndrome is a condition caused by a defect in metabolism resulting in bone deformity, an abnormally large head, a protruding abdomen and mental retardation. It was discovered by the 19th-century German paediatrician *G*. Hurler. Some of the symptoms of Hurler's syndrome are remarkably similar to the recentlyi

[6] Dr. Sidney Baker is a former faculty member of Yale Medical

School, where he received his medical and specialty training in paediatrics. Over the years he has gradually shifted from paediatrics and family medicine to treatment of adults and children with complex chronic illnesses. He has been at the forefront of medical research into discovering cures for some of the world's major, complex and most destructive diseases.

Chapter 11

The Human Prime Directive

"There is only one way to eliminate illness and disease, and that is to actually do something spiritual."—
Dr. Karina Halstead

Rather than provide you with another chapter that would only serve to further reiterate my findings, I would prefer to conclude with an important message from the mind of the heart. If we choose to live our lives in recognition of this simple premise, illness and disease will no longer be issues that control our lives. Hence, the first part is designed to heal the individual soul.

Healing and Transformation Part 1

- Listen to your body and understand its physical, emotional and spiritual needs.
- Live in the present, do not worry about the future, or hold onto the past.
- Take time to discover the eternal stillness of your heart and silence your internal dialogue.
- Stop looking for approval from others; you are the only judge that matters.
- Learn to deal with anger.
- Accept that you create your own world; the world 'out there' is merely a projection of your inner world.

- Do not be judgemental.
- Do not contaminate your body with unnatural toxins such as drugs and alcohol, animal flesh, and foods rich in refined sugar and carbohydrates.
- Forget old hurts and replace fear-motivated behaviour with love-motivated behaviour.
- Live your life in complete balance with the Earth and accept that you are interconnected with all of creation and the divine consciousness.

Interestingly, these twelve listed spiritual disciplines exhibit the esoteric planetary rulerships in the following order as listed: Sun, the Moon (the eternal lights), Mercury (the saviour), Venus (the morning star), Mars (the red planet), Jupiter (God almighty), Saturn (covenants), Neptune (the redeemer), Pluto (the last Adam), and Uranus (the mediator).

Healing and Transformation Part 2

"This the Elemental Spirits hear
In the East, West, North and South
May Human Beings hear it."—Rudolf Steiner

Thus far, the human prime directive has outlined the healing process necessary to heal the soul within the physical body. This second part outlines the healing and transformational process that is necessary to restore planet Earth to its former glory—that is the beautiful luminescent sphere free from violation, pollution and dis-ease.

Unfortunately, the cyclical problems that we are enduring upon this planet at this crucial juncture in our evolution are not improving; instead they continue to proliferate. Equally concerning are the tumultuous and deleterious consequences associated with illness and disease, especially those that are outlined in this book. These are not nascent concerns. The widespread effects of illness and disease have been responsible for wiping out civilisations over the course of millennia.

So, once again, we have arrived at a pivotal point upon the helical of evolution where the maladies of illness and disease have become a prevalent concern throughout the countless civilizations that frequent the Earth sphere. Yet again, a reverberating and disturbing prospect!

The issues of selfishness, illusion, despair and degradation that continue to portend our fragile existence are occurring because of the way a large percentage of the populace think—reoccurring thoughts set to the mode of negative are responsible for the extreme acts of violence, apathy and perversion that have been in effect for generations.

In order to save ourselves from epidemics and pandemics and our planet Earth from eventual cataclysm, we need to *think*, via the application of meditative techniques, from the heart-mind as opposed to the head-mind, meaning we need to *transubstantiate* (transmute) our thought patterns to the mode of positive. In order to heal ourselves completely we need to remember[1] to breathe in divine light and then send it out into the world, and into the negative field of energy that encompasses the Earth. We need to rediscover our spirituality and our divine heritage before it is too late.

Therefore, as humankind resides at the precipice of the approaching Aquarian Age, the time for action is NOW![2]

Being empowered by the light for the purpose of healing and transformation and then imparting the light to every corner of the Earth via a collective effort will effectively save us from self-annihilation and planet Earth from cataclysm. Unfortunately, there is no other way because we have exhausted our options at the physical level.

Endnotes

[1] I have used the word *remember* because we, as spiritual beings, know how to breathe in light directly from the source. Once again, it is because we have forgotten this fundamental fact. For

many breathing in the light will prove to be an unlikely, difficult concept simply because it is something universal that many of us have lost sight of. Through the application of free will, a large percentage of the collective have chosen to turn their backs on the divine in order to become engrossed in mankind's flawed illusion of physicality, because this is all they remember.

[2]For more information about *Healing* and *Transformation* please contact myself at: alanrichards59@gmail.com or alternatively go to www.josephspeaks.com

Chapter 12

A Guided Meditation: Healing the Mind, Body and Soul

"The meaning of life is to find your gift. The purpose of life is to give it away."—Pablo Picasso

A provocative quote from Picasso, and it is very significant of the twelfth house, the house of self-healing—healing the unconscious and subconscious.

The purpose of self-healing is to liberate the soul and relinquish the heavy burdens it has carried in the form of karma for millennia. Illness, in the form of dis-ease, is one such burden; but illness and disease are nothing but illusions, even if they appear to be very real in physicality. With the correct balance of elements such as nourishing the soul with God-light energy via breath meditation, positive thinking and the consumption of healthy nutrition, the physical body will rarely, if ever, succumb to illness and disease.

The final four chapters (9-12) were tailored with the aim of helping to prevent the prospect of illness and disease from ever becoming a reality. But before I begin this final brief chapter I would like to open with two profound quotations. The first is from a highly evolved soul from the spirit side of reality; and the second is from an evolving soul in physicality:

"It is no coincidence that so many beings—so many souls—are presently suffering with conditions that affect the heart centre and the physical heart, because the heart centre is under-nourished, it is under-considered, it is starved of the very energies that it is designed to give out; and your society is becoming reclusive. Yes, people seek other people, and they exist in crowds, in cities and societies, but they are terribly insular because they are not used to touching each other via the heart centre. A damaged heart centre also affects the body's hard drive — the brain centre. That is why there are so many physical and mental health issues on the Earth plane at present."—Joseph…Spirit Guide

"It may surprise you to be told that illness is created as a desire of the soul. How can this be? How can anyone desire to be ill? But they do…because they desire attention, they desire love, they desire to go through a process in which people are taking care of them. They desire to give in to the overwhelming belief that at some stage in their lives they will be ill."—Michael G. Reccia…Spirit Medium

Healing the Soul

Give a man a pill, and you mask his symptoms for a day. Teach him to meditate and he can heal his life. When he adopts a willingness to embrace his heart, he is enlightened and discovers the true meaning of his life and the purpose of his evolutionary incarnations upon the plane of physicality; a purpose accentuated by the karmic, cosmic and divine expressions of God.

The ingrained desire to communicate with the creator, God (the soul), is achieved through the process of silent contemplation or meditation. But to successfully communicate with God the physical body must be in a state of calm, undisturbed and secluded bliss, embraced by the eternal stillness of the heart.

Meditation is a process that reminds us of who we are—our true spiritual selves. Today, so many individuals no longer incorporate meditation into their daily lives simply because they have chosen to ignore their spirituality. Instead, the majority unconsciously favour irresponsibility, disillusionment and escapism, and the upshot of it all is that they leave in their wake disturbing ramifications. Peace and tranquillity are necessary to our survival; without them the proliferation of illness and disease upon our already troubled planet will only continue to accelerate.

This simple guided healing meditation has been designed primarily for the purpose of instilling peace, harmony and appreciation into the mindset of the individual. In addition, it has been created to remind the spiritual heart of its role in the pantheon of celestial creation. A deeper understanding of how to stave off any prospect of illness and disease (particularly dementia and depression) via the power of heart-mind transmutation will be successfully acquired. Remember, as spiritual beings on a physical journey, we possess the ability to bring every positive opportunity and negative pitfall into manifestation via the power of thought; and once we learn to heal ourselves we can then heal our planet Earth.

The Aspectual Visualization Technique

In order to successfully perform this meditative technique, enabling you to achieve your highest spiritual potential, turn your focus to a particular aspect in the natal chart that has an extreme significance to you. Try to remember that every aspect in the birth chart is significant in its own unique way. Then, close the eyes and visualise the color coordination of the associated aspect in the spiritual eye.

For those who are unaware of how to activate the spiritual eye, it is a relatively simple process: Place the thumb and forefinger on the soft fleshy indentation between the eyebrows, just above the bridge of the nose, remembering to hold the fingers firmly in place throughout the entire procedure. Once you have established this, close the eyes and take deep elongated breaths and imagine that you can "feel" each breath pulsating a designated color, and the spiritual eye will respond instinctively. As you grow more confident try to imagine each breath pulsating in multiple color co-ordinations. But please be aware that the spiritual eye is an extremely sensitive and powerful focal point of the psyche. Caution and common sense needs to be applied when activating this spiritually-aligned organ.

Remembering and thereby *feeling* each breath is a vitally important factor that emanates from God because the breath symbolises the life pulse energy of the soul. Every breath is a channel of divine light energy that purges the body of all negativity, sustaining the life force via its physical extant. Simple breathing exercises immersed in cosmic color co-ordinations, such as this planetary example demonstrates, consolidate your connection with your inner self, and with the divine.

A final important note: Please be aware that similar to all types of meditation the aspectual visualization technique can be likened to the germination process of a newly-planted seed. Try to remember that it is the water of devotion that helps the seed to germinate successfully. Therefore, in order to attain successful results, patience and determination are required.

Purging the Soul

During meditation the spiritual eye is activated and the newly-aligned chakras will often display their splendour and glory as mere background features. The colors of that all-important aspect will be the prominent feature; it's as if they are displayed in three-dimensional Technicolor.[1] This is because the aspectual colors and hues in the natal chart are important components in the chakral color spectrum, incorporated into the aura by the Lords of Karma, the Elders.[2]

If the proposed aspect is an opposition, let's say between the

Moon and Pluto for example, visualise the Moon merging its gentle energy with the intense energy of planet Pluto to create the purple lake/magenta that is indigenous to the opposition aspect (refer to aspectual colorations at the end of chapter). Then, as you continue to take deep breaths, visualise the synthesised colors of the aspect enveloping the body—ridding and cleansing it of negativity. Visualising planetary colors in this way increases chakral energy output so, in essence, they become more effective, otherwise chakras remain technically ineffectual.

An aspect such as a Moon/Pluto opposition signifies the liquefying of waste products as they are eliminated from the body. Equally, the opposition can create blockages in the body that over time causes intestinal dysfunction leaching the body of essential nutrients and minerals. Diseases such as irritable bowel syndrome, diverticulitis and Crohn's disease are commonly associated with an aspect of this magnitude. Visualising and breathing in the colors affiliated with these planets will limit the potential onset of these dis-eases, including depression and other depression related maladies, particularly if Saturn is prominent or afflicted in the natal chart.

The opposition is an extremely powerful configuration with the potential to harbour polarised tendencies—from conflict through to harmony. However, the opposition aspect does increase the range of possibilities that are open to the individual. The opposition denotes two possible outcomes: the threat of the proverbial sword, but more importantly the prospect of the potential handshake.

Unlike trines, which indicate talents that have been successfully honed in past lives, oppositions exemplify traits that have yet to be honed in the broadest sense of the word. Oppositions must be polarized in order to be honed, that way the opposition becomes the balanced polarity it is intended to be. If the opposition aspect remains unbalanced then it becomes an unyielding and unrelenting source of duality. On reflection, oppositions provide an opportunity to recognize and reconfigure the personalized image in the mirror—the reflection of our true self that we often fear. Oppositions coin the phrase: "two heads are better than one."

It is important to remember that when you perform this color breathing exercise for at least a 20-minute period each day, you will eventually (through spiritual realisation) attain the highest potential that your uniquely-personalised planetary aspect has to offer. It doesn't matter if the aspect or aspects you choose are deemed soft or frictional, the effects will essentially be the same depending on the aspect's purpose, and meditation is the only true means of activating trines and sextiles.

Thus, the aspectual visualisation technique is the perfect antidote for warding off illness and disease; and it is good for spiritual progression too because every planetary aspect in the natal chart accentuates a divine symbolisation of creativity, especially those I refer to as Predominant Healing Aspects (refer to Chapter 7 for more information).

Foremost Aspectual Colorations
- Conjunction (neutral): brilliant white
- Vigintile (progressive decile, higher-mind): gold
- Semi-sextile: deep pink
- Decile (higher mind): gold
- Semi-square: black and crimson red
- Septile (higher-mind): silver
- Sextile: emerald green
- Quintile (higher-mind): golden yellow
- Square: black and crimson red
- Trine: violet and royal blue
- Sesquisquare: black and crimson red
- Bi-quintile (higher-mind): golden yellow
- Quincunx: black and white[3]

- Quindecile: scarlet red
- Opposition: purple lake and magenta

Retrograde Aspectual Colorations
- Conjunction: ivory white
- Vigintile: honey gold hue
- Semi-sextile: pale pink carnation
- Decile: honey gold hue
- Semi-square: charcoal and scarlet red
- Septile: pale slate grey
- Sextile: apple green hue
- Quintile: lemon yellow hue
- Square: charcoal and scarlet red
- Trine: lavender and azure blue
- Sesquisquare: charcoal and scarlet red
- Bi-quintile: lemon yellow hue
- Quincunx: charcoal and ivory
- Quindecile: chocolate brown
- Opposition: amethyst and fuchsia pink[4]

Conclusion: Yin/Yang

The yin-yang polarity (symbolizing the balance between light and the dark) represents a perfect symbol of truth. In essence, a solar eclipse is a divine symbolization of the yin/yang polarity. According to the ancients, solar eclipses act as powerful significators and as reminders that through our free will we have the choice to walk the path of darkness; and in awe we can choose to be guided by the light. Lunar eclipses act as a kind of parameter between the light and the dark, instinctively drawing us ever closer to our chosen destiny.

Traditionally, the yin-yang polarity signifies harmony, balance, mediation, coherency, responsibility, transformation and absolution—the cornerstones of Universal Law. The ancient Chinese believed that it symbolized the key to understanding our spiritual heritage. As such it is a powerful aid for self-healing, and the yin-yang polarity can be implemented as a tool to assist in vision quests and a spirit guide in breath meditation—both for the purpose of awakening the inner spirit, the God within.

Finally, I wish to end simply by saying: "the cosmos (the beating heart of astrological law) symbolizes a quintessential blend of synthesized and synchronized energy particles (yin-yang) that emanate from a greater whole. Hence, the greater whole that is an important and integral part of evolution, and the foundation of Universal Law."

Blessings to humankind
In love and light
Alan R. Wheatcroft

Endnotes

[1] The new color chakras are an important theme of my book: *One Body Many illnesses, An Insightful Approach to Medical Astrology*, published by the American Federation of Astrologers

[2] A reference to the highly-evolved souls who orchestrate the karmic plan for the soul when it chooses a new physical life on the Earth plane.

[3] White is the neutral shade that essentially represents the doorway to infinity. Information about Aspectual Colorations is courtesy of the Akashic Records.

[4]Information about Retrograde Aspectual Colorations is courtesy of the Akashic Records.

"There are only two days in our lifetime that are shorter than 24 hours—the first day and the day we die.

One is celebrated every year, yet it is the other that makes us see living as precious. We should never forget that." (A Poignant Neptune affirmation)!—Dr. Kathryn Mannix, taken from her book *With The End In Mind*

Additional Publications by Alan R. Wheatcroft

One Body Many Illnesses, An Insightful Approach to Medical Astrology is available from AFA, www.astrologers.com, and Amazon.com.

Review from Mary Plumb

Alan Wheatcroft has written a distinctive book; its subtitle, *An Insightful Approach to Medical Astrology*, hints at an essential theme of its contents. Wheatcroft is an astrologer and spiritual healer who knows our physical bodies "as vessels of infinite light energy."

The connection between "Earth and the cosmos" has almost disappeared in modern times, and understanding and attuning to the energy of the specific light carried by the planets can make us all "capable of healing ourselves." This is a simplified introductory remark to a sophisticated book—as the back cover says, "Medical astrology is incredibly complex." Wheatcroft does not have a simple view of the subject; he goes beyond most medical astrology books and addresses "the intricate dynamics that are at work within the body; hence the spiritual, physical and the psychological interplay between the planets, the biorhythms and the chakras."

Before looking at conditions in the horoscope, the author describes how biorhythms (derived from the Moon and the planetary cycles) and the chakras are connected to periods when depletion in the energy system makes us vulnerable to disease. He offers examples throughout the book of how this works, and he suggests a website for calculating the biorhythms.

Wheatcroft's astrology is electric—he draws from many branches of the discipline—traditional (planetary dignities), midpoints, evolutionary, the presence of Algol, Black Moon

Lilith, minor aspects, etc.—but focuses on the nodal axis (and its rulers) to diagnose illness. There are fascinating case histories (e.g., narcissistic personality disorder, cardiovascular and lung disease, alcohol abuse, psychosis), all told with thorough astrological detail and with insights into not only the physical sequence of the disease, but also the spiritual and evolutionary processes at work. He delineates the horoscopes of Judy Garland and Patrick Swayze, looking at the timing of their illnesses and the causes of their deaths.

Although readers with a serious interest in medical astrology are the natural audience for this book, advanced astrologers who are drawn to healing and soul growth will be intrigued by the depth of Alan Wheatcroft's work as well. *One Body Many Illnesses* can be studied and contemplated on different levels: Along with quite specific medical details of the various illnesses in the case studies (including his own), the author also has ideas about the time and cause of death and the soul's experience in the bardo state.

Mary Plumb
Web and Book Editor for The Mountain Astrologer

Review from Donna Van Toen

Books on medical astrology are fairly rare. Good ones are rarer still. This is a good one, but you may as well be forewarned right at the beginning: It's not recommended for beginners, and Wheatcroft's system is incredibly complex. If you're not prepared to do a little work, chances are that you won't find anything here for you. The author is well versed in both traditional and modern astrology as well as evolutionary astrology, and he manages to synthesize the three very well, though some prior knowledge of each would be helpful if you're to make the most of the material presented.

The first portion of this book is on biorhythms and chakras. All of this material is new, and I must admit that it took me several tries to understand some of what he was saying once I got past the very thorough section on Astrological Influences and Effects, which for the most part was fairly familiar to me. The section of the Body's Hypersphere was pretty much beyond me. There is information there, but I was unable to use it. To do so, the author asserts, we need to use our third eye chakra and look deep within ourselves for answers, using guided meditation and color therapy. Since I have only a rudimentary knowledge of color therapy and not a lot of experience with guided meditation of this sort, I have left that for another time when I have more time to study and meditate. The list of hyperspheric colors will no doubt come in handy at that point.

I found the chapter on chakras easier to understand — and the fact that the author offered Patrick Swayze's chart for analysis was very helpful. I will note again, however, that this chapter is not devoid of new material. The author feels that at this time, chakras are in the process of changing colors. Additionally, he feels that five new chakras are being integrated into the psyche at this time. This material, and his explanation of the chakras with regard to health was very interesting, especially alongside the Swayze chart.

In contrast, the material on biorhythms was easier to use, though I did have to read it several times. This, by the way, could be a good system for timing and possibly identifying sources of illness. And I did find a couple of incidences where it was spot on with my own past history.

On the whole, I would like to have seen these sections expanded into one book with more detail. I get the feeling that the author could merely touch the surface of these fascinating subjects. And I would have liked more.

The three chapters on the Moon's Nodes are apt to be more accessible for most of you. There was plenty of excellent material here, including material on North Node and South Node transiting conjunctions. There is also a tie-in with traditional numerology in this section and a display of how the rulers of the Nodes can be strongly tied to various parts of the life path. This chapter alone is worth the price of the book.

The book ends up with case studies—cardiovascular and lung disease, bursitis, breast cancer, and even narcissistic personality disorder. These are not case studies of well-known figures, but they are very thorough and helpful.

Again, this is not the book for you if you're looking for a quick guide to medical astrology. Nor is it the book for you if you're closed to metaphysical principles. Otherwise, it's most definitely worth looking at.

Donna Van Toen
Book Editor for the International Society for Astrological Research

Review from Dulce Bell-Bulley

Congratulations on your well-researched and clearly written book *One Body Many Illnesses, An Insightful Approach to Medical Astrology*. It is truly a labor of love and wisdom. There is a lot to it! It is something to be proud of. Good job!

Dulce Bell-Bulley M.A. C.H.T.

Review from Maria Stiopei

This is a great book, rich in information; it's like a manual, which requires time and attention. I really enjoyed it. It is concentrated and straight to the point. Many of the things in it are new to me, and I would like to learn more about them, so I am hoping for a follow up. I am glad you opened up these concepts to me. Also, I have found by reading your book that it is very important to reenergise the body with universal energy.

I am very grateful having received this book directly from the author. If you're into astrology you'll certainly enjoy it. I highly recommend.

Maria Stiopei
strologer at Peregrine World

Review from Kira Sutherland

Alan's book takes you on a journey that goes beyond what most classical medical astrology texts cover. He introduces the basic principles of medical astrology and then takes the reader to another level of analysis by incorporating the biorhythms, the chakras and the Moon's Nodal soul story as key players in our health and occurrence of ailments.

This is a complex book that layers many ideas regarding the body and how they all interplay to increase or decrease our 'vital energy' and thus affect our health, ailments and energy levels. There is a spiritual theme throughout the book, with the emphasis on the soul's Nodal journey having a great impact on our health if we lose our way from what the Nodes are here to express in this lifetime. There are many great case examples that give the reader a good understanding of the interplay of these new ideas presented and how they manifested as ailments from a physical, mental or emotional starting point.

I come from a modern medical astrology background that incorporates the traditional aspects as well, and think Alan's book can add a great deal of insight and understanding for those wanting to work on a deeper level than just the physical aspects of astrology. I especially liked the use of the Moon's biorhythms and chakra systems to give a road map for the practitioner to investigate not just the physical aspects of disease but the emotional and spiritual dimensions as well.

Practical application is of paramount importance when working with medical astrology, as to tell the client all their health issues without guiding them on a journey of healing potential is a job only half done. Alan demonstrates and covers this second half of the healing process with great insight.

One Body Many Illnesses has many great case studies, where Alan clearly delineates certain illnesses using both the traditional alphabet of medical astrology and his added new techniques. There are instructions for how to calculate the biorhythms and directions to websites to assist in this matter. I especially like the array of differing case studies, not only focusing on physical ailments such as cardiovascular disease, pancreatitis, and lung issues but on personality disorders, alcohol abuse and psychosis.

The timing and description of Patrick Swayze's illness and eventual passing was a great example to understand the synthesis of Alan's techniques and to gain an understanding of timing of illness and a soul's journey through health and disease.

This is a book for those with a solid understanding of medical astrology and can lead the practitioner to new thoughts and insight as to why ailments may have presented themselves. It is a beautifully written book that doesn't just teach new medical techniques but leaves you pondering the inter-connection of the universe, one's soul and its necessary expression in the physical world.

Kira Sutherland
Australian naturopath, nutritionist, herbalist and astrologer.

Other Titles Published by the American Federation of Astrologers (AFA), www.astrologers.com

Astrology's Astro-Guide to Nutrition and Vitamins
    Lynne Palmer
An Introduction to Western Sidereal Astrology
    Kenneth Bowser
Blending Astrology, Numerology and the Tarot
    Doris Chase Doane
Black Moon Lilith
    Kelley M. Hunter
Biographical Dictionary of Western Astrologers
    James Herschel Holden
Classical Scientific Astrology
    George C. Noonan
Confidential Recollections Revealed
    Lambert Gustave-Brahy
Creative Step-Parenting
    Gayle Geffner
Cosmic Astrology
    June Wakefield
Contest Charts
    Doris Chase Doane
Designs for a New Age: Rectangles and Yods
    Alice Miller
Directions: Co-Detriments of Faith
    Reinhold Ebertin
Decanates
    Bernice Prill Grebner
Decanates and Duads
    Frances Sakoian
Delineation with Astrodynes
    Ken Stone

Delineation of Progressions
    Sophia Mason
Eclipses: Astrological Guideposts
    Rose Lineman
Forensic Astrology
    Dave Campbell
Finding the Person in the Horoscope
    Zipporah Pottenger Dobyns
Fixed Stars and Their Interpretation
    Hoffmann Ebertin
Fixed Stars and Judicial Astrology
    George C. Noonan
From One House to Another
    Sophia Mason
Finding our Way through the Dark
    Demetra George
Five Medieval Astrologers
    James H. Holden
Homosexuality in the Horoscope
    Karl Guenter Heimsoth
Horary Astrology and the Judgement of Events
    Barbara H. Watters
Health in the Horoscope
    Helen Adams Garrett
Have We Met Before?
    Emma B. Donath
How to Read Cosmodynes
    Doris Chase Doane
Horary Astrology
    W.J. Simmonite
Horoscopes of Africa
    Marc Penfield

Horoscopes of Latin America
 Marc Penfield
How to Handle Your Human Relations
 Lois Haines Sargent
History of Horoscopic Astrology
 James H. Holden
Horoscopes of Europe
 Marc Penfield
Horoscopes of Asia, Australia and the Pacific
 Marc Penfield
How to Give an Astrological Health Reading
 Diane L. Cramer
Horoscopes of the USA and Canada
 Marc Penfield
Harmonic Anthology
 John Addey
Intercepted Planets: Possibilities for a New Age
 Alice Miller
Interpreting Lilith
 Delphine Jay
Interceptions: Heralds of a New Age
 Alice Miller
Interpreting Empty Houses
 Ana Ruiz
Journal of Research of the American Federation of Astrologers
 James H. Holden
Jungian Symbolism in Astrology
 Alice O. Howell
Karma in the Horoscope
 Helen Adams Garrett
Lunar Nodes: New Concepts
 Bernice Prill Grebner

Lilith Ephemeris 2000-2050
    Delphine Gloria Jay
Medical Astrology for Healing
    Thaya Edwards
Mathesis
    Julius Firmicus Maternus
Minor Aspects Between Natal Planets
    Emma Belle Donath
More About Retrogrades
    Helen Adams Garrett
Modern Horary Astrology
    Doris Chase Doane
Modern Transits
    Lois Rodden
McWhirter Theory of Stock Market Forecasting
    Louise McWhirter
Money: How to Find it with Astrology
    Lois M. Rodden
North and South Nodes: Guideposts of the Spirit
    Cynthia Bohannon
On the Heavenly Spheres
    Helena Avelar
Prediction Techniques Regarding Romance
    …Ana Ruiz
Primer of Sidereal Astrology
    …Cyril Fagan
Planatary Powers: The Morin Method
    Patti Tobin
Progressions and Directions
    Charles A. Jayne
Progressions Directions and Rectification
    Zipporah Pottenger Dobyns

Planet-Centred Astrology
    Stephanie Jean Clement
Preface to Prenatal Charts
    Charles A. Jayne
Pagan Astrology for the Spirit and Soul
    Alice Miller
Potential Fulfilled: Accident Patterns
    Priscilla Gilbert
Paul of Alexandria: Introduction to Astrology
    James Herschel Holden
Rapid and Reliable Analysis
    Reinhold Ebertin
Relationships
    Helen Garrett Adams
Rhetorius the Egyptian
    James Herschel Holden
Stars Over England
    Marc H. Penfield
Self-Evident Astrology
    Jeffrey Sayer Close
Simplified Astronomy for Astrologers
    David Williams
Sex and the Outer Planets
    Barbara H. Watters
The Art of Forecasting Using Diurnal Charts
    Sophia Mason
The Lunar Nodes to Pars Fortuna: Journey and Goal
    Alice Miller
Transits
    Reinhold Ebertin
Transits and Solar Returns
    Ciro Discepolo

Astrology for Self-Healing   213

The 144 Doors of the Zodiac: The Dwad Technique
    Thyrza Escobar
The Degrees
    David W. Crowl
The Inconjunct: Natal and Transiting Aspects
    Frances Sakoian
True Crime Astrology
    Edna Rowland
The Mars Book
    Donna Van Toen
The Math of Astrology
    Peter Murphy
The Astro-Geology of Earthquakes and Volcanoes
    Lind Weber
The Progressed Moon Around the Zodiac
    Gisele Terry
The Contact Cosmogram
    Reinhold Ebertin
Transits
    Clara Darr
Transits and Planets
    Heber J. Smith
The Transiting Planets
    Frances Sakoian
The Astrology of Development
    Stephanie Jean Clement
The Progressed Horoscope Simplified
    Leigh Hope Milburn
The Introduction to the Science of the Judgements of the Stars
    Sahl Ibn Bishr
The Rulership Book
    Rex E. Bills

The Arabian Parts Decoded
   Lind Weber
The Text-Book of Astrology
   Alfred John Pearce
The Astrologer's Guide
   William Lilly
The Combination of Stellar Influences
   Reinhold Ebertin
Understanding Retrogrades
   Helen J. Adams
Unlocking Interceptions
   Helen Adams Garrett
Understanding Interceptions
   Chris McRae
Vocational Astrology
   Judith Hill
Why History Repeats
   Theresa H. McDevitt
Your Solar Return
   Cynthia Bohannon
Your Hidden Face: Projection in the Horoscope
   Tim Lyons

www.ingramcontent.com/pod-product-compliance
Lightning Source LLC
Chambersburg PA
CBHW071112160426
43196CB00013B/2550